THE BLACK COUNTRY AT WAR

ALTON DOUGLAS

CLIVE HARDY

DENNIS MOORE

ADDITIONAL RESEARCH BY JO DOUGLAS

© 1984 ALTON DOUGLAS, CLIVE HARDY, DENNIS MOORE, JO DOUGLAS.
© 1999 ALTON & JO DOUGLAS
Fifth Impression
ISBN No. 1 85858 133 8
Published by Brewin Books Ltd, Doric House, Church Street, Studley, Warwickshire. B80 7LG.
Printed by Heron Press, Unit 19, Bilton Ind. Est., Stockmans Close, Kings Norton, Birmingham B38 9TS.

CONTENTS

**The Destroyer, HMS Watchman, adopted by the Urban District of Brierly Hill in
"Warship Week", 22nd to 29th November 1941.**

ALTON DOUGLAS is probably best known as the author of several best-selling books and for the three years he was quizmaster (and co-writer), of the top-rated BBC Midlands TV series "Know Your Place". However, he has also been a TV and Radio character actor, professional comedian, showbiz/jazz book and record reviewer, TV and Radio commercial voice-over artist, 5th Royal Inniskilling Dragoon Guards trombonist, the voice behind several cartoons and children's toys, etc.

He has appeared in virtually every major theatre in the UK (including the London Palladium) and was responsible for hundreds of television warm-ups.

His television appearances include; "Know Your Place" (3 series), "Angels", "Seconds Out", "A Soft Touch", "Muck and Brass", "The Golden Shot", "The Knockers", "The Original Alton Douglas", "Nights at the Swan", "Watch This Space", "The Barmaid's Arms", "Open University", "Property Rites", "Big Deal", "Newshound", "Murder of a Moderate Man" and "The Bretts".
His Radio plays include "Mr Peabody and the Beast", "Troupers", "The Family That Plays Together, Stays Together", "You Can't Judge a Book by Looking at the Cover", "Sorry Goodbye and Get Stuffed" and the award-winning "Guernica".
He was also the archives and stills consultant for the centenary video "Made in Birmingham".

Since 1981 Alton has had over two dozen books published:

"THE BLACK COUNTRY AT PLAY"	"THE BLACK COUNTRY AT WAR"	"THE BLACK COUNTRY REMEMBERED"
"MEMORIES OF DUDLEY"	"MEMORIES OF THE BLACK COUNTRY"	"MEMORIES OF WALSALL"
"MEMORIES OF WEST BROMWICH"	"MEMORIES OF WOLVERHAMPTON"	"JOE RUSSELL'S SMETHWICK"
"BIRMINGHAM: A LOOK BACK"	"BIRMINGHAM AT PLAY"	"BIRMINGHAM AT WORK"
"BIRMINGHAM IN THE FIFTIES"	"BIRMINGHAM IN THE SIXTIES"	"BIRMINGHAM REMEMBERED"
"BIRMINGHAM SHOPS"	"MEMORIES OF BIRMINGHAM"	"BIRMINGHAM AT WAR VOL 1"
"BIRMINGHAM AT WAR VOL 2"	"BIRMINGHAM: THE WAR YEARS"	"DOGS IN BIRMINGHAM"
"COVENTRY: A CENTURY OF NEWS"	"COVENTRY AT WAR"	"MEMORIES OF COVENTRY"
"MEMORIES OF STRATFORD-UPON-AVON"	"MEMORIES OF SHREWSBURY"	"MEMORIES OF THE WREKIN AND BEYOND"

PRELUDE TO WAR

Saddled with a reparations bill of 136,000,000,000 gold marks, and plagued with economic problems, including the occupation of the Ruhr by French troops, 1923 was a year of crisis for the Weimar Republic of Germany. Such was the state of things that a relatively unknown 34 year-old political opportunist named Adolf Hitler attempted to overthrow the Berlin government. The whole undertaking was doomed to failure. Hitler had over estimated the degree of support for the Nazi party outside Bavaria. In fact the Nazis had no rating at all on a national level and were regarded merely as a paramilitary pressure group. But despite the failure of the Munich "Putsch", the Nazis credentials as a radical organisation were established and Hitler's subsequent trial and imprisonment gave the party the national publicity it needed.

Help for the tottering Weimer Republic came in the form of American investment, a drastic devaluation of the mark, and a modified method of paying reparations under the Dawes Plan. For several years Germany once again seemed to be heading along the road to prosperity, that is until 1929.

Between 1925 and 1929 the United States loans to Europe alone mounted to 2,900,000,000 dollars. American industry had grown rapidly since the end of the Great War due to a deliberate policy of readily available money by the Federal Reserve Bank. In July, 1929, this never-never land mentality was exploded when the supply of goods finally outstripped demand, necessitating a drastic reduction in output politely termed an inventory recession. Investors lost confidence and in less than three months 40,000,000,000 dollars was wiped off the value of shares on Wall Street alone. The impact of the Wall Street crash was felt world wide. Millions were thrown out of work and in several countries major banks collapsed.

It was partially out of the misery of unemployment and low pay for those fortunate enough to have jobs that National Socialism flourished. In the Reichstag elections of May, 1928 the Nazis secured 2.6 per cent of the vote, giving them 12 seats under the Republic's system of proportional representation. In July 1932 they polled 37.3 per cent of the vote, giving them 230 seats and making them the largest single party in the Reichstag. Despite his known dislike of the Nazis, President Hindenberg eventually had little alternative but to summon Adolf Hitler to the chancellorship. It was January 1933.

Hitler's first priority was to make his authority unassailable. On 28th February 1933 a decree was issued under Article 48 of the Constitution suspending normal civil liberties. In March came the Communist "plot" highlighted with the burning of the Reichstag. Hitler used the February decree to expel the 83 Communist members of parliament and concluded a deal with the Centre Party which gave him the necessary majority to pass the Enabling Law that empowered the Chancellor to issue legislation without having to seek the consent of the Reichstag.

Hitler now prepared to extend Nazi control and doctrine throughout Germany's institutions but he was quite willing to bide his time. However, it was not to be. The next stage in the Nazification of Germany was hastened by pressure from the Sturmabteilung (SA), the Brown Shirt paramilitary wing of the Party, which wanted to take over control from the army. Hitler seriously feared a military counter coup so much so, that he conspired with the high command to eliminate the SA leadership in the Night of the Long Knives (30th June 1934) in return for the direct backing of the army for his regime, and most important of all, an oath of loyalty to the person of the Fuhrer.

At Field Marshal von Blomberg's suggestion, the Fuhrer called the Commanders-in-Chief of his armed services to the Reich Chancellery at 4.30 p.m. on 5th November 1937. The subject was far too important for a large audience so the only member of the Cabinet present was Baron von Neurath, the Foreign Minister, and, apart from Colonel Friedrich Hossbach of the Wehrmacht, Hitler even excluded his five other adjudants. Industrial, economic, and munitions experts called by von Neurath got no further than the Chancellery smoking room, where they spent four hours before being dismissed without being called to give their opinions.

The problem was that the Nazis had reflated the German ecomomy so quickly that since the autumn of 1936 the country had been gripped with an increasingly severe shortage of iron and steel. Shortages were so great that in early 1937 the re-armament programme was cut back. For example the Luftwaffe needed at least 120,000 tons of steel a month to meet its arms production and civil defence programmes but was in fact receiving about 70,000 tons. The navy needed about 77,000 tons a month, was promised 45,000 tons, but in reality sometimes got less than 25,000 tons, with the result that the building programme of major surface ships fell behind schedule. The meeting ended with the navy being allowed an extra 20,000 tons for submarine construction.

There was a second part to the meeting. Hitler took the opportunity to inform his commanders of his aims for 1938. Speaking from prepared notes he told them that he was determined to solve Germany's Lebensraum "problem" by 1943 - 44 at the latest. Since Germany could not hope to become self-sufficient in food and raw materials she would have to look for them, the nearer to home the better, and if necessary to take them by force.

ANSCHLUSS AND CZECHOSLOVAKIA

Immediate plans were to be made for the unification with Austria — "Anschluss" — and the annexation of Czechoslovakia. Until now Germany's military planning had been defensive apart from Plan Otto, the invasion of Austria if the Hapsburg monarchy was restored. Göring suggested that Germany should disengage herself from involvement in the Spanish Civil War and Blomberg and Fritsch urged him to avoid war with Britain and France. Hitler however was convinced that Britain and France would do nothing about Austria and that they would abandon Czechoslovakia if it came to a showdown.

On 19th November 1937 Lord Halifax visited Hitler in Bavaria to discuss the possibilility of Germany obtaining colonies in Africa — probably at the expense of Portugal and Belgium, who were not consulted — in return for arms limitations. Hitler was unimpressed. He was not interested in African colonies which could be cut off in time of war. The empire he wished to create was along the ancient Teutonic path towards Eastern Europe.

By the beginning of 1938 Hitler was ready to move. On 12th February he invited the Austrian Chancellor, Kurt von Schuschnigg, to Berchtesgaden, the route lined intimidatingly with troops of the 120,000 strong Austrian Legion. Hitler was accompanied by Generals Richenau and Sperrle, neither of whom was noted for their good looks, and by the end of the meeting Schuschnigg had been pressured into including Austrian Nazis in his Cabinet. The question of Anschluss was raised, but no formal agreement reached. Hitler got the shock of his life a couple of weeks later when Schuschnigg announced that Anschluss would have to be decided by plebiscite. Fearing that the vote might go against unification, the German High Command improvised invasion plans during the night of 9th/10th March. Austria was annexed on the 12th, Berlin and France doing nothing to stop it.

On 20th February Hitler had given a speech in which he promised protection for all Germans living outside the Reich, a speech seized upon by Konrad Henlein and the Sudeten Nazi Party in Czechoslovakia to itensify their campaign for self-determination.

What was Great Britian's attitude towards the Reich? In

December 1937 Joachim von Ribbentrop, Hitler's ambassador in London, submitted a summary on British attitudes. It would not have gone unread. The excitable short-tempered Ribbentrop was one of only a handful of men Hitler trusted completely. In his report Ribbentrop stated that Britain now regarded Germany as her most deadly potential enemy and that Neville Chamberlain, who had been Prime Minister since 28th May, was in the process of formulating initiatives in the hope of purchasing peace in Europe. Britain would offer colonies and concessions on Austria and Czechoslovakia. However, he went on to warn the Fuhrer that while the majority of the British public was in favour of agreement with Germany, there was an "heroic" ruling class that in order to protect its own interests would not hesitate in swinging public opinion round in favour of war. Ribbentrop correctly predicted that Britain would make a secret offer to Germany in February or March 1938 but that Hitler must expect a tougher attitude in 1939 when British naval re-armament would be well advanced. Ribbentrop went as far as to suggest an Anglo-German Entente but in January, 1938 he had changed his mind. He wrote to the Fuhrer:
'I no longer believe in rapprochement. Britain does not want a Germany of superior strength in the offing as a permanent threat to her islands. That is why she will fight."

Appeasement, as Chamberlain understood it, required a settlement that involved concessions on both sides which would thereafter be honoured. Czechoslovakia was another matter.

On 28th/29th April 1938 the first of three Anglo-French conversations on German demands in Czechoslovakia took place. British policy towards the Czechs was ill-informed and unsympathetic. Czechoslovakia was not seen as a bastion to be defended but a "last chance for Anglo-German understanding." The British Cabinet had decided that Czechoslovakia was indefensible, and that nothing had been done to satisfy Sudeten German claims, by choosing to blatantly ignore the fact that since 1937 the Czech government had included three Sudeten German ministers. The French were bound by treaty to aid the Czechs if attacked. However, they feared that in the event of war they would be without British support. Outwardly the Anglo-French conversations were shown as the working out of a joint policy. In reality both governments had decided to abandon the Czechs, but a public announcement to that effect in London or Paris would have been political suicide. At all costs French honour had to be preserved.

On 21st April Hitler met with General Keitel and told him, "It is not my intention to smash Czechoslovakia by military action in the immediate future without provocation unless an unavoidable development of the political conditions within Czechoslovakia forces the issue, or political conditions in Europe create a particularly favourable opportunity which may perhaps never recur." On 15th May Konrad Henlein reported back to Hitler that the British Government was sympathetic to the Sudeten cause. Speaking in the House of Commons on the 24th March, Chamberlain had refused to widen Britain's obligations under the Treaty of Locarno to intervene if France got herself involved in a war with Germany arising out of her going to the aid of Czechoslovakia. Indeed Chamberlain saw no benefit to Britain of a free Czechoslovakia. Indeed, he shared Hitler's dislike of the Czech alliances with France and Soviet Russia, and another influence upon him was that the Dominions had little if any sympathy for a British guarantee to the Czechs.

On 20th May Hitler sent the draft orders for a pre-emptive attack (Plan Green) to General Keitel. The Fuhrer believed that any invasion of Czechoslovakia had to take place quickly so that Britain and France would not have time to react and within days Europe was gripped with the news that Germany forces were massing along the Czech border. To meet the threat the Czechs ordered a partial mobilisation. With 35 divisions the Czech army would certainly have given a good account of itself. However, the Czech government would not act without the promise of French, British, or possibly Russian military assistance.

On 4th September, the Czech President, fearing civil war, agreed to all Sudeten demands. On the 13th Hitler demanded self-determination for the Sudetenlanders. Within twenty-four hours rioting had broken out and Martial Law declared. Henlein fled to Berlin.

Hitler now took a gamble. Believing that Britain and France would still avoid a fight, he met Chamberlain and Sir Horace Wilson at Berchtesgaden and demanded the annexation of the Sudetenland. On the 18th the French Prime Minister, Daladier, came to London and agreed that those areas in which more than half the population were German should be ceded to the Reich. Hitler again set the pace by making 1st October the deadline beyond which military action would be taken. Chamberlain met Hitler again, and the Fuhrer, sensing victory, upped the price of peace by insisting that all military installations be handed over intact and a plebiscite carried out in all other areas with German minorities.

Chamberlain publicly stood his ground — enough was enough. War seemed imminent. On 23rd September Czechoslovakia mobilised, and with Britain pledging support for France in the event of a German attack on Czechoslovakia, Hitler realised that he had lost his chance to order a lightning attack. A conference was hurriedly arranged.

On 29th September the Munich Conference was convened, though neither Czechoslovakia nor the Soviet Union was represented. In the name of appeasement the result was a forgone conclusion. 11,000 square miles of territory, 3,000,000 Sudeten Germans and 700,000 Czechs were handed over to Hitler.

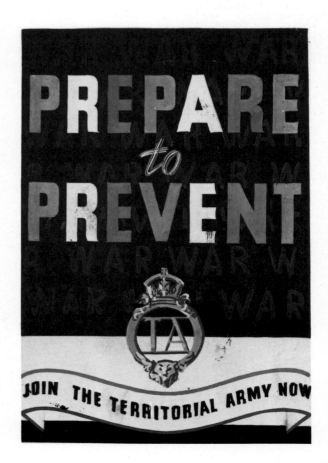

Hitler, followed by his staff, leaving the Fuehrerhaus. Munich Conference, 30th September 1938.

Of the conference, Hubert Masarik said, "Mr. Chamberlain yawned without ceasing and with no show of embarrassment. The atmosphere was oppressive for everyone present. It has been explained to us in a sufficiently brutal manner, and that by a Frenchman, that this was a sentence without right of appeal and without possibility of modification . . ."

If Hitler had been faced with the certainty of French and British intervention it is possible that his generals would have advised him not to invade Czechoslovakia. The Germans were short of munitions, fuel and trained reserves. Militarily the French could meet them on at least even terms and a successful invasion of Czechoslovakia would have depended on their destroying fortifications of which Albert Speer said " . . . a test bombardment showe that our weapons would not have prevailed against them."

In March, 1939 the Germans occupied the Czech provinces of Bohemia-Moravia and Memel, an action that finally convinced the Western Allies that in future they would have to act more firmly.

In a Reichstag speech on 28th April 1939, the Fuhrer listed the Czech military equipment that had fallen into German hands — 1,090,000 rifles, 43,876 machine guns, 2,175 field guns, 501 anti-aircraft guns, 1,589 aircraft, over 3 million shells, and 350 of the best tanks in the world, superior in guns and armour to anything in the Wehrmacht.

POLAND

On 24th March 1939 Britain and France agreed to resist German aggression against Belgium, Holland or Switzerland. One week later Britain said that she would stand by France in guaranteeing Poland's frontiers. On 3rd and 11th April, Hitler issued directives to prepare for an invasion of Poland.

On 26th January 1934 Poland signed a 10-year non-aggression pact with Germany. The Poles instinctively knew that one day they would have to fight and that the pact had bought them time. The problems began in earnest when the Nazi Party gained control of Danzig. There is plenty of evidence to suggest that the Poles were considering a pre-emptive strike against Germany but failed to get support from Britain or France.

Hitler, inspired by the lack of intervention over Austria and Czechoslovakia, decided that the time had come to settle the Danzig Question once and for all. He demanded the return of Danzig to the Reich with road and railway links in return for guaranteeing Poland's frontiers. The demands were rejected out of hand.

On 23rd May he told his High Command that Poland was to be attacked "at the first suitable opportunity" but that a war in the west had to be avoided.

On 20th August, the world was stunned by the news that the Soviet Union and Nazi Germany had signed a trade agreement. Hitler announced the formal annexation of Danzig and three days later concluded a non-agreesion pact with the Soviets. In secret session, Germany and Russia agreed to divide Poland and the Baltic States between them.

On the 24th Chamberlain sought American diplomatic help, though some confusion existed in the White House as to British intentions due to the hysterical reporting of events by the American ambassador in London. Kennedy gave the impression that Britain wanted Poland forced into unilateral concessions with the Nazis. In fact Chamberlain wanted the Poles to negotiate with Hitler in order to put him clearly in the wrong if he ordered an invasion, and if he did talk, to drag out negotiations until the winter rains came. Roosevelt's appeal to both sides to settle their dispute by direct negotiation or arbitration and the positive Polish response met British requirements.

Smethwick Fire Brigade & ARP enrol volunteers outside the Blue Gates Hotel, 19th March 1938.

Turnout of Dudley ARP services, May, 1939.

Digging trenches at Netherton, Czech crisis, 1938.

Wiretapping of the British and French embassies in Berlin and the decoding of telegrams by the Forschungsant meant that Hitler could follow hourly just how his enemies were reacting, and by 22nd August he had rightly deduced that while the western powers might well formally declare war they would not actually fight — not at first, that is.

Visualising a short campaign, Hitler ordered the invasion of Poland to commence at dawn on the 26th, but he was forced to rescind the order when Mussolini told him that Italy was in no shape to get involved unless she could be guaranteed massive military aid. On the 25th, the Fuhrer met with Sir Neville Henderson, British ambassador to Berlin, and informed him that he wanted a settlement with Britain and that he was prepared to guarantee the British Empire "with an offer" once the Polish question had been settled.

Between 26th and 28th August, the British Cabinet held a series of meetings to consider Hitler's message, but the government had no intention of repeating the folly of Munich, and went on to warn the Fuhrer that Britain was determined to stand by Poland. On the evening of the 28th Hitler took up the diplomatic initiative and asked Henderson "whether England would be willing to accept an alliance with Germany." The ambassador exceeded his instructions and replied that "speaking personally" he did not exclude such a possibility provided "the development of events justified it." In London, Henderson's response was considered political dynamite which, if leaked, would wreck Anglo-American relations.

On the evening of the 29th, Hitler announced that he would negotiate providing a Polish emissary arrived in Berlin by noon the following day. He denied that this was an ultimatum, for he hoped to divide London and Warsaw. He was convinced that if Chamberlain could be tempted by Anglo-German alliance then two possibilities might arise. Firstly the Poles might refuse to negotiate, in which case the British would be justified in revoking their guarantee. Secondly, if a Polish emissary went to Berlin and the talks broke down, then Chamberlain might refuse to fight on the grounds that the Poles had provoked war. Chamberlain to his credit had no intention whatsoever of being drawn into such a trap. He informed the Cabinet that the demand for a Polish emissary was unacceptable and that any Anglo-German agreement depended upon a just settlement for the Poles backed by international guarantees.

At 4.00 p.m. on the 31st Hitler decided that he could wait no longer, for winter would soon make an invasion of Poland impossible. With 1st September being the last favourable day for attack, he abandoned his attempt to split London and Warsaw and issued directives for the invasion to take place at dawn.

At 8.00 p.m. on the 31st the first German unit went into action when Sturmbanfuhrer Navjocks led an attack on a German radio station in Upper Silesia. His small force included a dozen convicted criminals dressed in Polish uniforms who were promised a reprieve for their co-operation. Having forced their way into the station, shots were fored and the "Poles" broadcast patriotic announcements. Once outside, the "Poles" were executed and left for the local police to find. Before the night was out, Eastern Europe was hearing reports of a Polish attack upon the Third Reich.

At 4.40 a.m. a German battleship bombarded Polish fortifications at Westerplatte near Danzig and one hour later German troops crossed the border in strength, the first serious fighting taking place in and around Gross-Klonia. Air raids were launched against Warsaw, Lodz. Cracow and Poznan, but met with stiff resistance from the Polish Air Force. With only 159 fighters to defend the entire Polish air space, the PAF resorted to head-on attacks that shredded the nerves of many German pilots, forcing them to break formation and shed their bombs wide of the intended targets. Obliged to challenge as many Luftwaffe incursions as possible, the PAF lost irreplaceable fighters and its strength gradually whittled away.

The Polish Army had about 30 divisions in the field and 10 in reserve areas against the 60 Wehrmacht divisions under von Brauchitsch. French dithering at making a statement of intent had induced the Poles to delay mobilisation with the result that they were overwhelmed in many sectors before reserves could be brought up.

On the afternoon of 1st September Britain ordered general mobilisation and the Defence Regulations, including the "blackout at sunset", came into force.

On the 2nd, Norway, Sweden, Denmark, Finland, Iceland, Latvia and Estonia declared neutrality, and Italy and Japan both declared their intentions not to take part.

When Neville Chamberlain came to the despatch box at 7.30 p.m. he must have felt a lonely man indeed. He was virtually isolated, his supporters falling away on all sides. He had made desperate efforts to secure a lasting peace with Germany and even at this late stage he told the House that a conference could be convened if Hitler would withdraw his troops. But appeasement was no longer a diplomacy that satisfied public opinion or the practicalities of diplomacy. It had failed.

Chamberlain sat down to a silent House which broke up in some confusion. Chamberlain's Cabinet, which had probably been the most docile this century to its Prime Minister's wishes, felt that war could no longer be avoided. Sir John Simon went to see Chamberlain and told him of the Cabinet's wishes and that war must be declared at once. The Anglo-French ultimatum was delivered to Berlin at 9.00 a.m. on Sunday 3rd September, asking for an assurance that German forces would suspend their advance into Poland and declaring that if no such assurance had been received by eleven o' clock then a state of war would exist. At 11.15 a.m. Chamberlain broadcast to the nation. No assurance had been received. "Consequently this country is now at war with Germany." An hour later the dejected Prime Minister spoke to the Commons. "This is a sad day for all of us, but to none is it sadder than to me. Everything that I have worked for, everything that I have hoped for, everything that I have believed in during my public life, has crashed into ruins."

To many, the policy of appeasement is seen as something unique to Neville Chamberlain. This is not so. It can be detected in our foreign policy from the second half of the nineteenth century onwards, and in a way was the only course open to a nation that was both economically stretched and trying to defend a far flung empire. Neville Chamberlain was following the political traditions of the previous seventy-five years, the difference being that none of his predecessors had had to contend with a political opponent as aggressive, as opportunist, or as fanatical as Adolf Hitler.

First Aid demonstration.

Demonstration of babies' gas mask, Walsall.

HIS "BATTLE" NEED WORRY NO ONE

"DARLING, THE PAPERS DISTINCTLY SAID ARSENAL OPENED FIRE AT WOLVERHAMPTON TODAY!"

HOME, SWEET HOME

West Bromwich Town Hall, registering for evacuation. "Mothers with children under 5 years who wish to be evacuated should attend the nearest elementary school in the evacuable area at any time after 2 p.m. today Saturday 2nd September 1939", (the day before war was declared). ▷

THE HOME FRONT

War was officially declared at 11 a.m. on Sunday, 3rd September 1939, but the earlier crisis in 1938 saw feverish activity which gave much needed practice in the field of ARP (Air Raid Precautions).

Then trenches were dug in parks, school playing-fields and other open spaces: these soon became waterlogged and as the international tension seemed to ease, they were eventually filled in and levels restored. During this 1938 crisis, Dennis Moore remembers: "Within the school time-table, we were transported from the Wolverhampton Municipal Secondary School to spare factory workrooms in Great Brickiln Street and taught to assemble civilian gas-masks. Stretching those thick rubber-bands over the filters left us all with raw thumbs for weeks afterwards. How many we assembled (and correctly too!) must have amounted to thousands, but we were never told. Stocks of emergency coffins were also prepared but, thankfully, we did not have a hand in this."

A well known chemical plant manufacturer tells: "The War Office asked us to supply 'gas' containers in large quantities. What sort of 'gas' referred to was not revealed to us, so, just before war started, we made and transported the containers (empty) to Thornton Cleveleys in Lancashire where, for safe keeping they were buried under the sands".

The diarist of Walsall's Blue Coat C. of E. School, Miss E. Farrington, wrote:

Sept. 1st 1939	War clouds gather more thickly and notice was received today that pupils in certain districts will be evacuated and that all schools will close this afternoon until further notice.
Jan. 31st 1940	No coke for boilers. Children sent home.
Feb. 26th 1940	School attendance now compulsory after being on a volunteer basis for twelve weeks.
May 14th 1940	No parents took up the option to have their children evacuated.
Aug./Sept. 1940	Air raid warnings most nights.
Aug. 17th 1940	Air raid alarm p.m. Only a few children arrive at school. They sang "There'll Always be an England" in the playground. Wish Hitler could have heard them.

All the famous Black Country brewers continued to produce a mild and a bitter beer throughout the war, but since grain was mainly used for food, the gravity of the beers was of an indeterminate nature. In fact the brews were quite palatable even though the mild became affectionately known as D.D.T. No, not the pesticide, it meant "Died Drinking Tenpenny". This beer was ten old pence (approx. 4 new pence) per pint!

The people of Walsall were used to seeing the green livery of the Wolverhampton Corporation's trolley buses travelling to their town via Willenhall but were goggle-eyed to awake one morning to see yellow buses on their streets. These vehicles bore on their sides BOURNEMOUTH CORPORATION and carried destination boards BOSCOMBE and PIER. Having been evacuated from the south coast (to avoid the possibility of damage by tip-and-run raiders), several were later badly damaged and had to be replaced before the whole fleet was returned. In addition, 2 or 3 London Green Line single-decker diesel buses were evacuated to the West Midlands.

The staff of James Beattie Ltd. organised a Fowl Club on the store roof to produce eggs for sharing amongst the whole staff.

Because, after Dunkirk, many more of our Continental Allies were based near Wolverhampton, the same store employed an interpreter.

Enemy prisoners of war were employed on local farms, for example in Trysull. The Italians were considered lazy and spent their time making baskets, whilst the Germans, with their own brand of sabotage, knocked the shoots of the seed potatoes before planting in order to ensure a poor crop.

Assembling gas masks in Walsall.

Bournemouth Corporation trolley bus No. 130 along Cannock Road. Wolverhampton had 12 Bournemouth buses, also some crews.

Walsall Corporation bus No. 222. Note the white line painted on the mudguards and masks and on headlights. 29th August 1943.

RAY WILSON (Rushall)
Conductors were issued with a kind of flash lamp with the light shining downwards so that you could see the coins you were receiving and tickets issuing. This you fixed either to your uniform lapel mainly, or onto your straps, whichever preferred."

Waiting for the Bridgnorth bus. Stay-at-home holidaymakers queue for the five hour round trip from Wolverhampton.

Scouts from Halesowen present a mobile canteen to the YMCA, the ceremony taking place in the Royal Mews, Buckingham Palace, June 1942.

WARTIME
money saving
RECIPES

WARTIME recipe: Beg one egg. Borrow three tea-cups of flour. Steal half a pint of milk from neighbouring doorstep. Add a wine-glass of corporation water and a pinch of your own salt. Mix well, and leave in a slow oven for one hour. The result is a Yorkshire pudding as big as a sofa cushion. Serve hot with roast beef, if available. Failing roast beef, use as second course with as much butter and sugar as you can wangle.

Nourishing
High Tea and SUPPER
Dishes

There's a real art in serving the right sort of last meal, whether it's High Tea or Supper, especially in wartime. It should be well-balanced, satisfying but not stodgy, and sufficiently nourishing to repair the day's wear and tear on nerves and tissues. It should include either a raw salad or correctly cooked vegetable dish, and one of the body-building foods: cheese, dried egg, bacon, meat or fish; with bread, cake or scone as 'fillers'. Here are some High Tea and Supper recipes that win on all counts. Try them and see how well they go down.

TWO COMPLETE MENUS

(1) Salmon Savoury, Watercress & Beetroot Salad, Bread, Margarine, Jam or Marmalade.

(2) Pilchard Pancakes, Raw Vegetable Salad, Bread, Margarine, Jam or Marmalade.

SALMON SAVOURY

Ingredients : 4 level tablespoons flour, quarter pint water, 3 heaped tablespoons salmon (quarter lb.), ½ teaspoon mixed herbs, 1 teaspoon vinegar, salt and pepper. *Quantity:* Enough for 4. *Method :* Mix flour with a little of the water. Bring remainder of water to boiling point, add to flour paste and allow to boil for 5 minutes. Then add salmon, herbs, vinegar and seasoning to taste. Pour on to slices of toast and place under a grill for 2 minutes. Serve with salad of beetroot and watercress. To finish the meal, serve bread and margarine, with jam or marmalade.

PILCHARD PANCAKES

This dish is not only savoury but satisfying.

Ingredients : 1 lb. potatoes, 2 pilchards, mashed, 1 tablespoon chopped leek, 2 tablespoons chopped parsley, 1 dried egg, reconstituted, pepper and salt. *Quantity :* Enough for 4. *Method :* Peel, cook and mash potatoes, add pilchards, leek, parsley, dried egg and seasoning. Mix all together and drop dessert-spoonfuls of the mixture into hot fat. Brown on both sides. Serve with raw vegetable salad and follow up with bread, margarine and jam or marmalade.

Try this different recipe, too :

SOUR-SWEET CABBAGE with SAUSAGE-MEAT CAKES

Ingredients : 1 lb. cabbage, 1½ level teaspoons salt, 1 oz. bacon fat or dripping, 6 tablespoons vinegar, 1 level tablespoon jam or sugar, 2-3 cloves, 1 lb. sausage meat. *Method :* Cook the cabbage in a little boiling salted water till tender. Strain. Boil the bacon fat, or dripping, with the vinegar, jam or sugar and cloves for several minutes. Strain, and pour over the cooked cabbage. Serve with sausage meat divided into cakes, and fried slowly on both sides till cooked through.

ECONOMISE WITH POTATOES until the new crop arrives.

THIS IS WEEK 40 — THE LAST WEEK OF RATION PERIOD No. 10 (April 1st to April 28th)

THE MINISTRY OF FOOD, LONDON, W.1. FOOD FACTS No. 251

DOLLY ALLEN
(Black Country Night Out Commedienne) *"It was a cold winter's morning and there was a long queue waiting for our fruit rations, when a large car drew up by the shop and a woman in a fur coat stepped out. She must have been pregnant, which allowed her to walk right in without waiting. She was served with her fruit and went, then a woman who was also in the queue shouted 'Can I come in? I'm stagnant.' We laughed at her and she said, 'Yow con loff, but this'll be six.' Somebody shouted, 'Yow must like having kids with this lot on,' and her answer was, 'Well yow caut get anough ter ate. Yer got a fill yer bally up we summut.'"*

They will get Turkeys by Halves
—With Luck

By Daily Mail Reporter

BUTCHERS worried by the barrage of orders for Christmas turkeys are putting customers' names down for half a bird each.

◇ **A practical demonstration of field kitchen cookery given by the WVS at Monmore Green greyhound track, 30th July 1941.**

FOOD FACTS

EASTER AND ETCETERAS

The children need not wait until after the war for a taste of the novelties which used to brighten our pre-war Easters. These Easter recipes include some special ones for the younger members of the family.

Be sure to get in a packet or so of Dried Eggs before the holiday, especially if you expect visitors. They're a wonderful standby, and you'll need them for making some of these suggestions.

EASTER PIE
is savoury and tempting

Ingredients : 1 lb. mixed root vegetables, 1½ oz. dripping or lard, quarter pint water, salt and pepper, quarter lb. sausage meat, 3 dried eggs, reconstituted. *Method:* Cut vegetables into small dice and fry in the fat until well browned — about 15 minutes. Add the water, season well and bring to the boil. Place in a piedish. Roll the sausage meat into small balls, and place among the vegetables and bake in a moderate oven for 15 minutes. Season eggs and beat. Pour over the vegetables, return to the oven and bake for a further 10-15 minutes, until the egg is set and browned.

SOYA MARZIPAN PASTE
Ingredients : 2 oz. margarine, 2 tablespoons water, 1-2 teaspoons almond essence, 4 oz. soya, 4 oz. sugar. *Method :* Melt margarine in water. Draw saucepan off heat, stir in almond essence, sugar and soya. Turn out, knead well and shape into little eggs and chicks.

BIRDS' NESTS
Make pastry tartlet cases in the usual way, and when cold fill with tiny soya marzipan eggs, some plain, some rolled in cocoa. Little cress baskets, filled with small marzipan eggs and chicks, and tied with ribbon, also make attractive nests.

SIMNEL CAKE

Good for Easter too. This recipe is not as difficult as it looks

Ingredients : 4 oz. margarine and lard, mixed, 3 oz. sugar — brown if possible, 2 level tablespoons treacle or syrup, 8 oz. plain flour, pinch salt, 2 level teaspoons baking powder, 1 level teaspoon cinnamon, 1 level teaspoon mixed spice, 4 dried eggs, reconstituted, ¾ lb. mixed dried fruit, ½ teaspoon lemon substitute, milk to mix, soya marzipan paste, reconstituted egg for glazing. *Method :* Line a 7-in. cake tin with greased paper. Cream fat and sugar and beat in the treacle or syrup. Mix flour, salt, baking powder and spices, and add to the creamed mixture alternately with eggs. Add the dried fruit and lemon substitute and mix to a fairly soft consistency. Place half the mixture in the cake tin and spread evenly. Add a round of soya marzipan paste ¼ in. less in diameter than the cake tin and place the remaining cake mixture on top. Bake in a moderate oven for 2 hours. Next day, cover the top of the cake with a thin layer of soya marzipan paste. Brush lightly with reconstituted egg and brown slightly under the grill or in a very moderate oven. Decorate with small eggs, chickens, etc., made from soya marzipan.

Bottling Bitter Oranges for Marmalade later on

Bottle this pulp NOW for making marmalade when you have saved up enough sugar.

Wash 6 Seville Oranges, put into a pan with 2 pints water. Simmer gently for 2 hours with a lid on the pan. When cool enough, cut up the fruit, separating the pips. Return pips to the water in which the fruit was cooked. Boil for 5 minutes. Slice the fruit, and place with the liquid strained free from the pips, in a pan. Bring to the boil, pour into hot preserving jars. Seal immediately, and where the screw band is used, give it a half-turn back to allow for expansion. Place jars in a pan of boiling water to cover jars completely; bring to the boil and boil for 5 minutes. Remove one by one and tighten the screw band. Next day, remove clips or screw band and test the seal.

When required for marmalade, empty the pulp into a pan and bring to the boil. Add 3 lbs. of sugar, stir until dissolved, and boil rapidly until setting point is reached.

LISTEN TO THE KITCHEN FRONT TUESDAY, WEDNESDAY, THURSDAY & FRIDAY at 8.15 a.m.

THE MINISTRY OF FOOD, LONDON, W.I. FOOD FACTS No. 247

⬆ Waste collected by Walsall school-children for pig food. Councillor A. E. Hurst (Chairman of the food collection scheme) inspects a day's contributions, April 1941.

Immediately following Dunkirk, May, 1940, place names were removed to confuse enemy paratroops. Dudley Arms Hotel, Market Place, ⬇ Dudley.

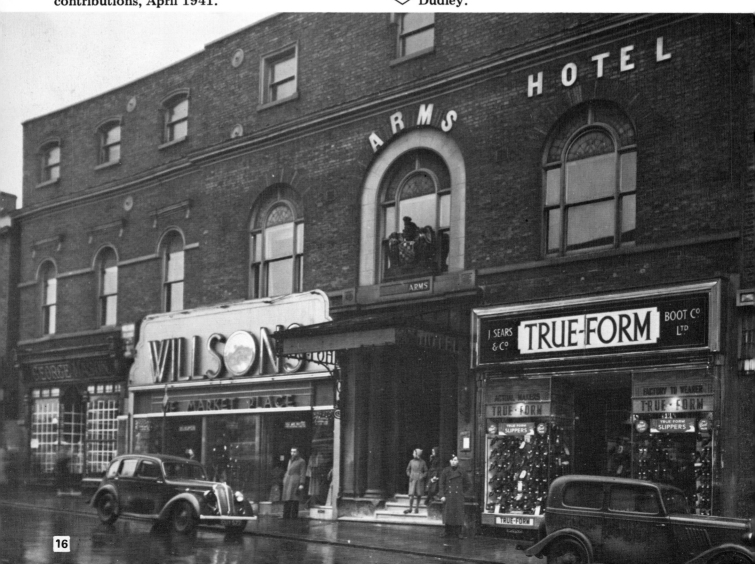

HINTS ON SAVING FUEL.

HOW TO MAKE COAL LAST LONGER.

Dissolve a tablespoonful of common salt in ½ pint of water and sprinkle this over a small scuttleful of coal. The coal will not burn away so quickly and will give a steady red glow.

HOW TO LIGHT A FIRE WITHOUT WOOD.

Take a whole sheet of newspaper, roll it from corner to corner, and then roll it round the finger and tuck the end in. (Neither of the rollings should be tight.) Lay the fire (lightly) in the usual way, using about five of these paper "lighters" for a sitting-room grate, and seven for a kitchen stove.

KEEPING THE FIRE IN.

1. Waste paper, torn up, damped and rolled in an old newspaper, which should also be damped, makes a first-rate economiser of coal. A sitting-room fire can be kept in for many hours by putting such a roll down at the back of the grate with a shovel of slack over it and two or three good lumps of coal in front.

2. Small coal or slack, sawdust, and clay may be mixed together until they are about as thick as mortar. The mixture should then be moulded into convenient brick-like shapes, afterwards leaving it to dry; or the slack can be mixed with sawdust slightly moistened with paraffin and shaped into balls as big as an orange. You cannot light the fire with such bricks or balls, but they will keep a fire going a long time, and will give out strong heat if placed at the back of a grate with coal in front.

3. Large lumps of chalk give out a great deal of heat if placed in a fire which has already been started some time. The chalk becomes as red and glowing as coal, and lasts a considerable time, thus saving much firing.

4. A handy way of keeping the fire in is to take a shovel of slack, turn the tap on it for a second or two, and to place it at the back of the grate. Two or three shovelfuls so applied will keep a fire in for many hours.

THE ECONOMY OF USING GAS COKE.

Gas coke and coal mixed in equal parts will give a steady, hot, red fire. The more coke is used the more there will be of the materials needed for making explosives for the Army and Navy.

◁

Mrs. Churchill, wife of the Prime Minister, opens a garden fete at Himley, August 1944.

16-year-olds registering for duties with the Girls Training Corps. Behind the recruits are some well-established members who are acting as guides and messengers. ◁

C ♔ D
CIVIL DEFENCE

BLACK-OUT TO-NIGHT
11.4 p.m. to 4.57 a.m.
Sun rises, 5.42 a.m.; sets, 10.19 p.m. To - morrow: Sun rises, 5.42 a.m.; sets, 10.20 p.m.
Moon rises, 9.8 a.m.; sets, 12.30 a.m. to-morrow.
Rises to-morrow, 10.9 a.m. Full Moon, June 28
Lights up, 11.19 p.m.

YOU WILL WRITE OUT 50 TIMES JONES MI' "I CANNOT HAVE PICTURE POST UNLESS I *ORDER* IT"

Men and women are needed <u>now</u> in the
CIVIL DEFENCE CORPS

The Duke of Kent inspecting Civil Defence Cadets at Dudley, 1940. ⟹

Members of the ladies section, Wolverhampton CD volunteers, loading a van with cooked food for the schools, 17th December 1943. ⟱

Protecting the Hippodrome, Queen Square, Wolverhampton, 1939.

The Police Station, High Street, West Bromwich, 1939.

20

A light-hearted off-duty moment in the Police Station yard at Tettenhall, 1942. (Cell window at top of picture.)

40 mph Speed Limit Call to all Cars

THE Government is to ask all drivers to observe a 40-m.p.h. limit in order to economise in petrol, Lord Templemore informed the House of Lords yesterday.

He was replying to questions about the "high and uneconomic" speeds at which Government vehicles were driven.

Lord Templemore said the 40-m.p.h. limit would be an appeal instead of an order, because an order would not be enforceable without an increase in police supervision, and the use of fast cars which would cause waste.

The fighting Services were issuing instructions, added Lord Templemore, that their cars should not under ordinary circumstances be driven at over 40 miles an hour, and all civil Government departments were to issue instructions forthwith that cars under their control were not, save in exceptional circumstances, to be driven at speeds exceeding 40 m.p.h.

Complement of Women's Auxilliary Police Corps at Tettenhall, 1942. ⇩

⇩ Goodyear Special Police, 1940

Issued by the Ministry of Home Security.

WHAT TO DO ABOUT GAS

OTHER COUNTRIES LOST THEIR FREEDOM in this war because they allowed the enemy to create confusion and panic among their civilian population so that the movement of defending armies was impeded.

We are not going to allow that to happen here. It won't happen if we are all on our guard, prepared to meet anything the enemy may do.

He may use gas. THE DANGER IS NOT SERIOUS if you do the right thing, both NOW and when the time comes. If you do, this weapon will have failed and you will have helped to beat it.

Here are the things to know and do. Read them carefully and remember them well in case the day comes. Keep this leaflet and look at it again.

HOW NOT TO GET GASSED.
NOW

1. In your gas mask you have the best possible protection against gases that affect your lungs or your eyes. It is a sure defence if you use it properly and in time. Make sure your own and your children's gas masks fit and are in working order : your warden or A.R.P. post can tell you. Practise putting them on and get used to wearing them with confidence. Your life may depend on whether you can put your mask on quickly. Remember to take off your spectacles before putting on your gas mask.

2. CARRY YOUR GAS MASK ALWAYS, and have it handy at night.

3. To prevent the face-piece misting over, smear a little soap lightly on the inside once a week.

4. If your chemist has " No. 2 Anti-gas ointment " (price 6d.) in stock, buy a jar. Read the instructions on the jar and carry it always. This ointment is for use as a protection against the effects of liquid blister gas.

IF THE GAS RATTLES SOUND.

1. PUT ON YOUR GAS MASK AT ONCE, wherever you are, even in bed.

2. TAKE COVER. Get into any nearby building as soon as you hear the rattle. Go upstairs if the building is a tall one. Close all windows in your house.

Don't come out or take your gas mask off till you hear the handbells ringing the " Gas clear ".

NEVER LOOK UPWARDS—you may get a drop of liquid gas in your eyes.

COVER YOUR SKIN UP so long as you are out of doors—hands in pockets, collar turned up. Or if you have an umbrella, put it up.

IF YOU DO GET GASSED.
GAS OR VAPOUR. If you breathe any gas or vapour—

1. PUT ON YOUR GAS MASK AT ONCE.

2. KEEP YOUR MASK ON, even though you may still feel some discomfort.

3. If the irritation is serious and does not stop after a time, apply to the nearest A.R.P. warden or member of a First Aid Party.

LIQUID BLISTER GAS. If you are splashed with liquid gas from a bomb, and you can see the dark splash on your skin or clothing you must act as follows :—

SKIN.

(*a*) Dab, NOT wipe, as much of the liquid off your skin as you can with your handkerchief ; then rub " No. 2 Anti-gas ointment " well into the place. Don't forget your handkerchief has become very dangerous—destroy it.

(*b*) If you haven't the ointment by you, go to the nearest chemist's shop, where you will find bleach cream and be told how to use it.

(*c*) Ointment or cream should be put on within FIVE MINUTES of your being splashed. If this is impossible, wash at once with soap and water, preferably warm—this may save you a bad burn.

CLOTHING.

(*a*) Take off any splashed outer garment AT ONCE, before the liquid soaks right through to the skin—seconds count.

(*b*) If you are within five minutes of your home or any private house or other place where you know you can get a wash, go there and wash yourself. Before going in, take off your shoes and *any* clothing which you think the liquid has splashed—your health matters more than your feelings.

(*c*) If you can't get to such a place within five minutes ask the wardens or police what to do. They will know where the public cleansing centres are.

KEEP YOUR FOOD SAFE FROM GAS

1. Poison gases will not always affect even exposed foods to such an extent that they become dangerous for human consumption, but in any case very simple precautions will protect your food entirely.

2. Food in cans or airtight bottles is perfectly safe, and flour, rice, tea, butter, etc., should be kept in tins or jars with well-fitting lids. Refrigerators are very good protection. Perishable foods would be safe in them, or in a gas-proof room. Store all your tins and jars in cupboards or in places where they cannot be splashed by liquid gas.

3. If there is any risk that your food or water may have been contaminated, on no account attempt to deal with them yourself. Notify the police or an air raid warden. Your local authority will give expert advice and treatment.

WE CAN BEAT GAS ATTACKS
—if we know what to do, and do it.

MRS. BETTY RUSSELL

"I remember an occasion in late 1940/early 1941 when serving as a member of the ARP decontamination squad. I was on duty along with other ladies of the squad at Tower Street Baths in Walsall. The whole team retired to bed due to lack of activity, when during the night the air raid sirens suddenly set off their customary wail which was quickly followed by the sound of aircraft overhead. The duty officer immediately ordered everyone to get up and be ready, and the whole unit hurriedly got dressed and made off to their appointed stations, but some of the ladies found to their embarrassment that as they tried to put on their tin hats the rather inflexible metal chapeaux resisted all attempts to be placed on the ladies' heads — due to a barricade of hair curlers still securely in position on each respective female head!"

⬆ **Decontamination squad.**

⬇ **Decontamination exercise.**

Wolverhampton ARP Report Centre.

AIR RAID PRECAUTIONS

Worcestershire County Council

AIR RAID PRECAUTIONS

This is to certify that the Bearer
George Richard Humphries
has been appointed as an Air Raid
Warden. This is his authority to carry
out the duties laid upon Wardens by
the County Council of Worcestershire.

Geoffry Ince

Ibium Clerk, Clerk.
STOURBRIDGE

Date of issue of card *25th Sept '40*

Date of appointment
of Warden. *20th Sept '40*.

Signature of Warden *Geo R Humphries*

F1353

Dame Beryl Oliver, Head of the Nursing
Detachments of the British Red Cross, watches Dr.
Barton, Surgical Officer of Walsall General
Hospital, taking blood from donors. Lady Dorothy
Meynell is seen in the background. 10th May 1943.

GENERAL INFORMATION

GOODWIN'S INFORMATION BUREAU

Our staff of Experts who contributed to this book are ready to help you to solve your problems, not only with cooking but any of the other subjects in this book. Send a 2½d. stamp and Baby Picture cut from a bag of Goodwin's Extra Self-Raising Flour, together with your queries and an individual reply will be sent to you by return of post.

Identity Cards

You must carry your Identity Card wherever you go. If you do not you may find yourself at the Police Station! Children of school age should *not* carry their Identity Cards, which should be signed and retained by the parents, but should carry their name and address on their person (in the case of very young children a label should be sewn to some part of their clothing).

Only the Police and members of the Armed Forces on duty have the authority to require you to produce your Identity Card for inspection.

WAR-TIME COMMONSENSE

Do you know the positions of all the Air Raid Shelters in your locality?

In case of an aerial combat always keep indoors, for fear of falling shrapnel, bullets, etc. (and falling Heinkels).

Don't pick up shrapnel until at least half an hour after it has descended; if you do it will be so hot as to surprise you and you will have a very permanent souvenir.

Coal can only be purchased from merchants with whom you are registered.

Do you keep a flashlight handy at night?

Be careful to point a flashlight towards the ground at night, and walk with it held rigid, not swinging with the arm, so that it dazzles oncoming traffic.

It is always wise to check the times of your train service, etc., every now and again as they alter so frequently.

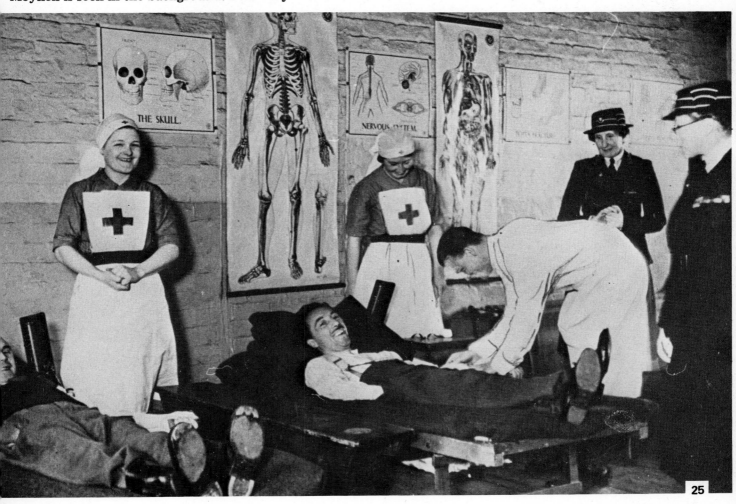

National War Savings Efforts 1939 — 1945.

These notes on Halesowen would be incomplete without special reference to the efforts made by the people of the Borough and the splendid results of the various Campaigns.

" SPITFIRE "

The first effort was the gift of £5,000 for the purchase of a Spitfire, and the Log Book shows that it commenced its operational career in April 1942 and was engaged upon fighter sweeps, bombers' escorts and convoy patrol. On one occasion the squadron attacked a goods train at Le Treport and left two engines damaged, and on another the Squadron escorted bombers to attack targets in occupied France; it was attacked by a formation of Me. 109 planes, of which two were shot up and the others disappeared into the clouds. On another occasion four FWs. attacked the Squadron and endeavoured, unsuccessfully, to break through the fighter cover and two enemy aircraft were destroyed. The report states: " These are just a few examples of the fine work that your Spitfire has done. In August 1942, after taking part in an air attack on targets in occupied France, it was shot down. Short though its career was, it left behind a grand record of which the donors can feel justly proud."

**'WAR WEAPONS'
WEEK
April 1940.**

A Target of £150,000 was fixed and it was considered fairly large for a Borough of this size and odds were laid against it being reached. To everyone's amazement, delight and satisfaction everyone's amazement, delight and justifiable pride, the target was more than doubled—nearly trebled—when the final result shewed that over £410,000 had been raised.

**" WARSHIP "
WEEK
March, 1942.**

No doubt encouraged by the huge success of the previous campaign (yet wondering whether sufficient time had elapsed for " stockings " to be refilled) the Halesowen Savings Committee bravely fixed the target at £310,000. Until practically the last day of the Campaign, however, it seemed their optimism had been too great, but hard work put in by everyone enabled the Campaign to reach the grand total of £330,000. As a result the destroyer H.M.S. Achates was adopted by the Borough.

On the 31st December, 1943 the ship, adopted by the Borough, was engaged in convoy duty to Russia and sunk, but the Savings Committee—with the same commendable pluck—immediately started a campaign to replace her although the date for Wings for Victory Campaign had already been fixed for May 1943. The people of Halesowen Borough rose nobly to this appeal which raised £241,482. Only three or four places in the whole country, who had lost their adopted vessels, had courage enough to launch such an appeal.

**" TANKS FOR
ATTACK "
July to Sept., 1942**

No particular target had to be set for this Campaign, but everyone was asked to increase his or her savings during this period by a percentage over the savings of the corresponding period of the previous year—and this was done.

**" WINGS FOR
VICTORY " WEEK
May 8 to 15, 1944**

This appeal followed so quickly on the last that the pessimists seemed to be right when a Target of £240,000, representing six heavy bombers, was fixed by the Savings Committee. It was only little more than a month since the last appeal had been made, yet the response can only be described as truly magnificent for the grand total of £258,482 was reached.

**" SALUTE THE
SOLDIER " WEEK
June 24 to July 1,
1944**

Just as the sailors and airmen had had their weeks, so the soldier had his. The Target set this time was £275,000, which was certainly an optimistic one. The Target was, for the fifth time, exceeded and the total realised was well beyond expectations, the final figure reached being £352,404.

In all these efforts grateful thanks are due to the members of the Halesowen Savings Committee, Street' Group Secretaries, Women's Voluntary Services, Works Organisers, and all others who assisted, and last, but not least, to the general public who so splendidly came forward with their savings for the good of the country, the Borough and themselves. The total invested in the Borough during these campaigns was £1,688,368, and the total savings since the inception of the War Savings Campaign in November 1939 to the end of August 1945 is £3,592,735.

" THANKSGIVING SAVINGS " WEEK, October 6th to 13th 1945.

The Campaign fixed for the above week is one of thanksgiving for the victory over Germany and Japan.

The Target has been fixed at £200,000. **The result — will be what you make it.**

The proud war savings achievement already mentioned **must** not be allowed to go by default. **Let this be " our greatest hour."**

SAVINGS

The 1914 — 1918 war saw a patriotic surge by the citizens of Britain to save money by lending it to the Government in order to finance a war — the birth of War Savings. The earliest forms, of what was to become during 1939 — 1945 National Savings, were savings stamps, quite literally postage stamps stuck onto a card. When the 6d. savings stamp came along, ironically it bore the emblem of the swastika, but this was quickly changed.

Throughout the land, savers thronged to their post offices, Trustee Savings Banks, Savings Kiosks and Banks to buy savings stamps, National Savings Certificates, 2½% National War Bonds, 3% Savings Bonds and 3% Defence Bonds. The slogan was "Lend to Defend the Right to be Free."

Tireless efforts by voluntary collectors took the various campaigns into the very homes of the public and the co-operation given by schools and industry meant total coverage.

Special local efforts in the Black Country took the form of "Warship Weeks", "Wings For Victory Weeks", "Spitfire Weeks", etc.

Dudley held a "Wings For Victory Week" from 29th May 1943 to 4th June 1943 when the target was £500,000, which could buy, would you believe, 100 Spitfires! In the event, the amount raised was £725,000. A novel promotion was mounted at certain Sellings Centres in the town when George Formby, the stage and film comedian, and his wife, Beryl, donated twelve 15/— (75p) Savings Certificates to people named George and Beryl who bought National Savings securities nearest to a specific time. George was currently appearing at Dudley Hippodrome.

Twenty Spitfires (£100,000) in Sedgley's "Wings for Victory Week" held from 8th to 15th May 1943 was the target; £120,192 was raised. The log-books of these aircraft purchased were to be kept and presented to the Council after the war.

Tipton's special week in 1943 set a target of £250,000 and had subscribed £188,000 in the first five days. The town justly boasted of 119 Savings Groups at this time.

Wednesbury's aim was also £250,000 at the end of June 1943.

The War Savings Committee for West Bromwich revealed that industrial Savings for the six months to 31st March 1945 totalled £31,279, subscribed by workers at Braithwaites, J. Brockhouse & Co., Hamstead and Sandwell Park collieries, Kenricks, Geo. Salter & Co., Walsall Conduits, Wellington Tube and others.

From 16th to 23rd November, 1940, Wolverhampton's "Navy Week" set a Savings target of £1,000,000, enough to purchase two destroyers. Achieved: £1,140,314. Later, in March 1942 the town 'adopted' the cruiser HMS Newfoundland (Capt. Ravenhill, RN) which formed part of the Allied fleet in Tokyo Bay in August, 1945 to accept the Japanese surrender.

Bearing in mind today's inflation, the above figures must be considered colossal in 1940's terms.

Those very people who saved money also saved by being shrewd and frugal. Newspapers had been considerably reduced in size anyway, and often were no more than four pages long. Nonetheless householders conserved the sheets either for compressing into fuel or for collection by the local authorities for re-cycling. Such was the result that official forms often bore the scattered print images of a previous existence.

Food was not to be wasted, bearing in mind the considerably risks taken by the Royal Navy and Merchant Navy to bring it to these shores, so the scraps left after meals could be put into conveniently placed pig-swill bins, so providing nourishment for many Black Country porkers.

Right at the beginning of the war, housewives were urged to hand over their aluminium pots and pans for raw materials needed to build aircraft. The resultant metal was later considered sub-standard and the scheme was abandoned.

Apart from irreplaceable memorial gates, metal was won by removing all other iron fences and gates to melt down for gun-metal and armour-plating. The Black Country was a major contributor in this respect.

Water had to be pumped to houses and factories and the coal for raising steam to drive the pumps was precious. Householders were implored not to fill their baths above a very meagre level. Even Buckingham Palace complied.

Silver paper formed an integral part of wireless sets for the armed forces so it was not long before it became a scarce commodity. West Bromwich collected it with fervour and did the same with empty toothpaste tubes which were reconstituted to provide further new tubes.

Wool from discarded pullovers and socks was unwound and re-knitted by the hard-working ladies of Quarry Bank and Brierley Hill to provide new socks, gloves, scarves and balaclava helmets for the troops. Other items provided were blankets and hot-water bottle covers needed at civilian emergency centres.

A dodge in Wolverhampton and elsewhere to prolong the life of torch-batteries was to pop them into the hot oven for a few (repeat few!) minutes.

Most coal users knew that coal sprinkled with salt dissolved in water would prevent the coal burning away too quickly and would assure a steady glow. Families gathered into one heated room in the house and listened to wireless in the dark. No TV then, of course.

A lady from Kingswinford still proudly displays her hay-box which she used right through the war to complete the cooking of partly-cooked food. To cook without fuel was quite an achievement and so patriotic.

Potatoes and carrots dominated many meals, and indeed Woolton Pie (named after the Minister of Food, Lord Woolton) seemed to the youthful stomach to be all potato and carrot. "Dig for Victory" was the slogan of the time.

Not all swimming pools were open to the public and those that were did not have the luxury of heated water, but somehow we did not seem to mind.

Two Bradmore families offered to preserve eggs at glut times for neighbours by submerging the eggs in an isinglass solution. The result, regrettably, was slightly unfresh musty-tasting eggs.

A ramble into Baggeridge Woods, Gospel End, Sedgley, was not just healthy exercise. During the walk, Mum and the children gathered fallen branches and small logs to take home, thus augmenting their coal or coke allocation. Dad was either away in the Forces or resting between shifts.

The Marsh & Baxter Ltd., factory at Brierley Hill was fully extended to produce the delicacies the pig could provide: ham, bacon, pork, trotters, chitterlings, scratchings, fry, faggots, liver and lights, etc. Every bit of the pig was utilised: the bristles sterilised for brushes; the squeal for referees' whistles! Offal was not on official ration, so queues formed everywhere whenever there was a rumour that a butcher had some available.

With ration books, coupons, points, dockets, chits or whatever, the whole country was in a mood for conservation, making-do and mending, re-constituting, re-hashing (call it what you will) and it was this mood of Savings which did, in the end, contribute so much to final victory.

A Messerschmitt, brought down "somewhere in England", raised £500 for Dudley's Spitfire Fund, October, 1940. Henry Hall, the famous bandleader, along with his musicians, assisted at the opening of the exhibition.

Defence Bonds.

Defence Bonds, like Savings Certificates, can be bought at any of the places mentioned. Each Bond costs £5.

You may buy any number of these Bonds to a total value of £1,000, even though you may already hold 500 Savings Certificates. So may every member of your family.

Interest is paid on Defence Bonds at the rate of 3 per cent. per annum. It is not added to the value of the Bond, as in the case of Savings Certificates, but is paid to you twice yearly on 1st May and 1st November without anything being deducted for Income Tax. (If you pay Income Tax you must show the interest you receive on your Bonds in your Income Tax returns.) Your interest will be posted to you in the form of a warrant; but if you prefer, it will be paid direct into your Account in the Post Office Savings Bank or a Trustee Savings Bank.

You can cash the Bonds at any time by giving 6 months' notice, and you then get back the money you paid for them, together with whatever interest is due to you since the last payment. If you hold the bonds for 7 years you will receive when you cash them £1 0s. 0d. premium for every £100. But in case of necessity you can cash the Bonds on special terms by giving a few days' notice.

Post Office Savings Bank and the Municipal Bank.

You may deposit 1/- and upwards in the Post Office Savings Bank or in any Trustee Savings Bank.

Interest is added to your Account.

You can withdraw your money easily and speedily.

Full information can be obtained at any Post Office or at the Municipal Bank.

YOUR MONEY LENT TO THE NATION IN ANY OF THE WAYS DESCRIBED IN THIS LEAFLET IS ABSOLUTELY SAFE, BECAUSE THE STATE GUARANTEES BOTH THE SECURITY OF YOUR CAPITAL AND THE PAYMENT OF YOUR INTEREST.

* * *

* * *

THE ENGLISH.

If an earthquake were to engulf England to-morrow, the English would manage to meet and dine somewhere among the rubbish, just to celebrate the event. *Douglas Jerrold.*

Brierley Hill
URBAN DISTRICT
WINGS FOR VICTORY
TARGET
£210,000
Inaugural Luncheon
April 17th, 1943.
Chairman : Councillor LEN HICKMAN, J.P.
(Chairman, Brierley Hill "Wings for Victory" Week Committee)

SAVE & LEND FOR VICTORY

MAKE YOUR MONEY FIGHT

We want weapons and yet more weapons of defence and attack. Save and lend to pay for them now.

A Bomber Aircraft costs approximately £20,000
A Fighter Aircraft costs approximately £5,000
We want you to LEND—not give—the money to provide:-

SIX BOMBERS	.. ..	£120,000
SIX FIGHTERS	.. ..	£30,000
	TOTAL	**£150,000**

This seems a lot of money to find doesn't it? It would be if it had to be found by one or two people, but there are 37,000 of you in Halesowen who can do something towards it. If every one of you did what you could we could find **SIXTEEN BOMBERS AND SIXTEEN FIGHTERS**.

Do your share so that you can ask your friends whether they have done their whack.

Every penny and pound in war savings is a hammer blow for victory.

Now then "Play up Yeltz!" "Hommer 'em Cradley!"

This is to certify that the

Merchant Navy Comforts Service Week

which took place in the

Borough of *Winton Regis*

from *16th September* to *23rd September 1944*

provided the sum of £ *3000 2 5*

for Emergency Rescue Kits, Prisoner-of-War Parcels, Comforts, and other Services for the Officers and Men of the Merchant Navy

The Chairman and Management Committee wish to place on record their grateful thanks to all those public minded citizens who gave their time and money in paying this practical tribute to the Officers and Men of the British and Allied Merchant Navies

Chairman · ·) *National Headquarters,*
Hon. Treasurer } *Canfield, Essex*
Appeals Director : *Appeal Headquarters,*
62, Heath Street,
London, N.W. 3

DESIGNED BY PETER GAUVAIN

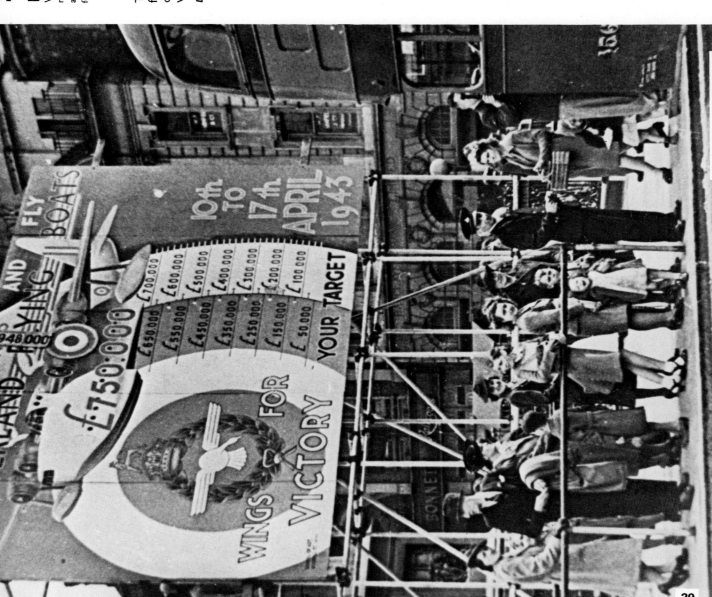

The Bridge, Walsall.

Smethwick War Weapons Week, December, 1940. An exhibition of photographs, aeroplane parts, etc., held in the Central Newsroom, High Street, raised £532,250.

"SERVE IT UP HOT!"

Hot work, this . . hotter than serving coffee and sausage rolls. "Coffee, sir—and two 'am sandwiches, yes sir, ninepence sir." That was yesterday. To-day, it's shells . . and more snells . . softening up the Nazi positions with steel. Salute his courage . . his endurance. SALUTE THE SOLDIER! Match his fighting spirit by saving—right up to the hilt! Let your increased savings be a token of your gratitude . . your respect . . your admiration . . for the glorious soldier of Britain.

Issued by the National Savings Committee

Col. K. J. Martin, DSC, takes the salute at the opening of Sedgley's Salute the Soldier Week, 17th April 1944.

31

Salvage depot at Wednesbury. The Mayor of Wednesbury, Councillor Whitehouse, and the Chief Sanitary Inspector, Mr. F. J. Turner, examine old high-tension batteries, while on the platform in the rear women helpers are stacking bales of paper. August 1941.

Thousands of metal pots and pans being salvaged for the aircraft industry. July, 1940.

Civil Defence Comforts' Fund Flag Day, 28th May 1941.

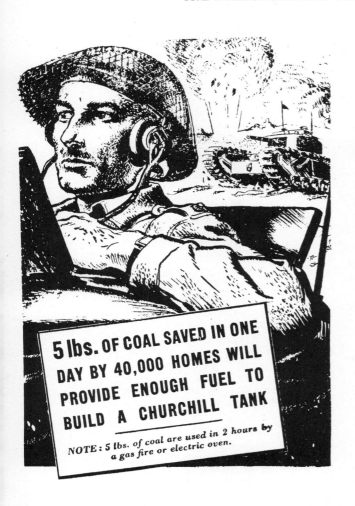

5 lbs. OF COAL SAVED IN ONE DAY BY 40,000 HOMES WILL PROVIDE ENOUGH FUEL TO BUILD A CHURCHILL TANK

NOTE: 5 lbs. of coal are used in 2 hours by a gas fire or electric oven.

IF 50 PEOPLE DON'T TRAVEL

1 TANK CAN

At this most important time
Needless travel is a "crime"

BRITISH RAILWAYS
GWR — LMS — LNER — SR
UNITED TO WIN THE WAR

INDUSTRY AT WAR

The industrial might of the Black Country played a vital role in the nation's war effort. Thousands of firms large and small alike were called upon to divert much of their capacity to armaments production to such an extent that in individual firms it accounted for anything up to 90 per cent of output. Such is the complexity of this topic that in a book of this type we can give only a brief insight into the contribution made.

As the re-armament of the late 1930's gathered momentum, Black Country firms were called upon to play a part. In 1937 the prototype Boulton Paul Defiant turret fighter made her maiden flight and in 1938 tank production began at Metropolitan-Cammell's Old Park Works, with a batch of 45 A.10 cruisers. Opened in 1939 for the production of 3.7 inch anti-aircraft shells, New Crown Forgings Ltd. of Wednesbury was equipped with specialist machinery made by the Wellman Smith Owen Organisation of Darlaston and was the prototype for shell forging plants in Canada, Australia, India, and at a later date the United States of America. That same year Accles & Pollock of Oldbury had caused a stir at the World Trade Fair by claiming that they could manufacture the smallest diameter steel tube in the world. The Americans would have none of it and sent what they considered to be the smallest tube in the world to A & P only to be shot down in flames when A & P promptly put another tube inside and sent it back!

The Wellman Smith Organisation continued to develop and manufacture machinery and furnaces for shell production. Wellman-made equipment, could produce in excess of 350 3.7 inch anti-aircraft shell forgings per hour and by the end of the war some 80,000,000 shells had been produced on their machines, using 2,125,000 tons of steel. Wellmans also manufactured bridge-laying equipment as well as machinery for the Mulberry harbours and the Pluto pipeline and maintained a continuous output of steel smelting furnaces, gas producing plant, cranes, shot furnaces, etc.

By mid-1942 Metropolitan-Cammell's production of Valentine tanks had reached its peak of 82 a month, a total of 2,135 being built over a period of 3½ years and the construction being divided between their Midland and Old Park Works. Concurrently with the Valentines, Old Park built 435 Churchill heavy infantry tanks together with a further 185 hull assemblies for other firms, and a batch of 75 Cromwell tanks armed with a 77mm high velocity gun. Other war production included light tanks, armoured cars, artillery trailers, pre-fabricated hulls for tugs and light tankers. The production of railway equipemtn continued but on a much reduced scale.

John Thompson (Wolverhampton) Ltd. produced a vast range of equipment including galvanising baths, annealing covers and salt baths for the aircraft industry, about 5,765 naval mines, 1,200 air cover intakes for tanks and 3,100 gun pedestals. In April, 1944 they were asked to build 36 landing craft, each capable of carrying a 30 - ton tank or several smaller vehicles. They also built about 900 Haslar smoke units, some of which finished up in North Africa, and another export was a number of rail-mounted coal-fired mobile power stations for the USSR.

Thompson's motor pressings plant produced thousands of vehicle frames, gun mountings, bomb containers, and the aero components subsidiary was sub-contracted by Vickers Armstrong to work on the exhaust systems, heating and rudder components for the Wellington bomber. At a later date the subsidiary was involved on the sub-assembly of the meteor jet fighter. Over at Dudley Thompson's manufactured bouys and lockgates for boom defences, scammell frames for tank transporters, petrol and oil tanks, power station equipment and the incubators and vacuum concentrator for Britain's first large-scale industrial plant for the production of penicillin.

At the precision tube manufacturers Accles & Pollock the 3,500 workforce produced rifle barrels, flash eliminators for automatic weapons and structural framing for Lancaster bombers. In fact there was A & P tubing somewhere in every British-built military aircraft of World War II — 120,000 of them. Another A & P product was hyperdermic needle tubing, quite literally produced by the mile.

Steel making capacity was stretched to the limit. At Stewart & Lloyds, Bilston, furnace tapping lit up the night sky so much that ARP black out precautions were abandoned as impracticable.

In March, 1942 the Secretary for Mines, David Grenfell, told the House of Commons that 140,000 miners had left the industry since the declaration of war. M.P.'s of both sides pressed for the immediate recall of miners from the forces but the army objected, claiming that this would seriously affect the fighting efficiency of many regiments. In December 1943 a system of balloting for conscripts to enter the mines began. As youngsters became of age for the forces, one in ten was forced into the mines. Some 21,000 young men served as Bevin Boys, so called after the Minister of Labour, Ernest Bevin, but only about a third were up to the exacting standards required for working underground. The scheme failed in that it actually contributed to a fall in production.

⤴ Camouflaging of the Boulton Paul Aircraft factory is almost complete. In the foreground are Blackburn Rocs freshly built within the factory. The famous Boulton Paul gun-turrets are prominent on the aircraft.

CHARLIE BLACKOUT

"I spent the early days of the war painting roof skylights with black paint and camouflaging many of the factories. The only problem was that when the war finished I had to go round stripping all the paint off again!"

A breathtaking aerial view of the Boulton Paul Defiant taken over the Belvide Reservoir near Brewood. The formidable armament in the gun-turret wrought havoc with German planes, especially at the time of Dunkirk.

The Huns later realised there was an undefended blind-spot beneath the Defiant and exploited this.

The Defiant ended its days, sadly as a target-towing aircraft for the training of new RAF ⤵ pilots and air-gunners.

⬆ King George VI and Queen Elizabeth visit Boulton Paul. The King is speaking to Sir Stafford Cripps, Minister of Aircraft Production.

The presentation of a silver salver on behalf of Boulton Paul to Flt. Lieut. S. R. Thomas, acting Squadron Leader of the Defiant Squadron which, at Dunkirk, shot down 37 enemy aircraft in one day and destroyed 100 enemy aircraft between May, 1940 and November, 1941. 23rd December 1941.

Newly-built and camouflaged, these petrol bowsers stand outside Thompson Bros., Bilston ready for delivery to the R.A.F.

It would be few years later before the gas-lamp near the bridge would once again give light to a peaceful Black Country scene.

Miss Elsie Dale (a former barmaid) of Pa[r]
Lane, Fallings Park, Wolverhampton [was]
Chief "go-getter" in a West Midlands "[G]
To It" factory where she beat Birmingha[m]
girl Evelyn Duncan for turning out An[ti]
Aircraft shell components. She produce[d]
6,018 in one week against Miss Duncan[s]
6,000. 1st October 1941.

ROCKET PROJECTOR

BAILEY BRIDGE PARTS

MOBILE BRIDGING PONTOON OVER 1,000 MADE
AIRBORNE TRAILERS OVER 1,000 MADE

AIRCRAFT PARTS

STIRLING LANCASTER STIRLING

MOSQUITO

VALVES FOR CYLINDERS & DISTRIBUTORS

JUST A BIT OF OUR 40,000 TON EFFORT

OERLIKON GUN MOUNTING

1,000 OF THESE TRAILERS

JAMES GIBBONS LTD
WOLVERHAMPTON

James Gibbons Ltd.,
Wolverhampton.

Haslars in action.

Churchill Tank with flame-thrower components manufactured in the Black Country, August 1944.

39

◁ Tanks under test at Metro-Cammell.

◁ One of the many products made at Guys of Wolverhampton.

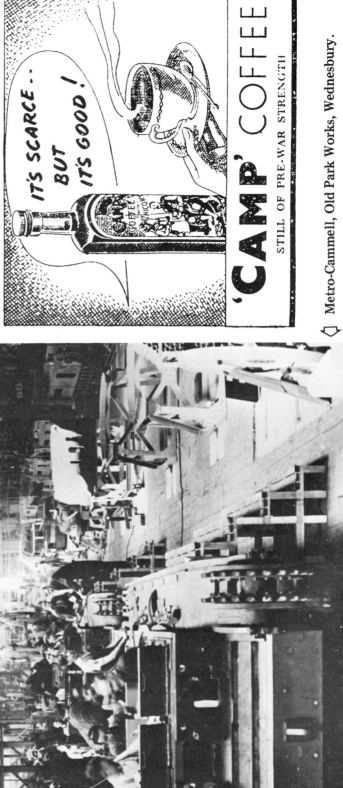

⇩ Metro-Cammell, Old Park Works, Wednesbury.

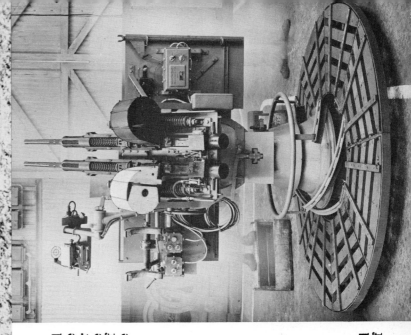

War workers at a Walsall tank factory celebrate the production of yet another tank. This particular vehicle will soon be in the hands of the Tank Corps men in the picture, 4th October 1941.

⇦

⇦ Light anti-aircraft gun and platform. Note 2 pairs of ghostly feet!

M.P.s Told 'No Rationing of House Coal'

'SAVE FUEL' CAMPAIGN INSTEAD

A MINER was sent back from the Army to the pit a miner's M.P. told the House yesterday. Five days later he was killed at the coal face. The accident took place at noon, and then (said the speaker) "the colliery company, which clamoured for this man" to come back, deducted half a day's wages for the day he was killed."

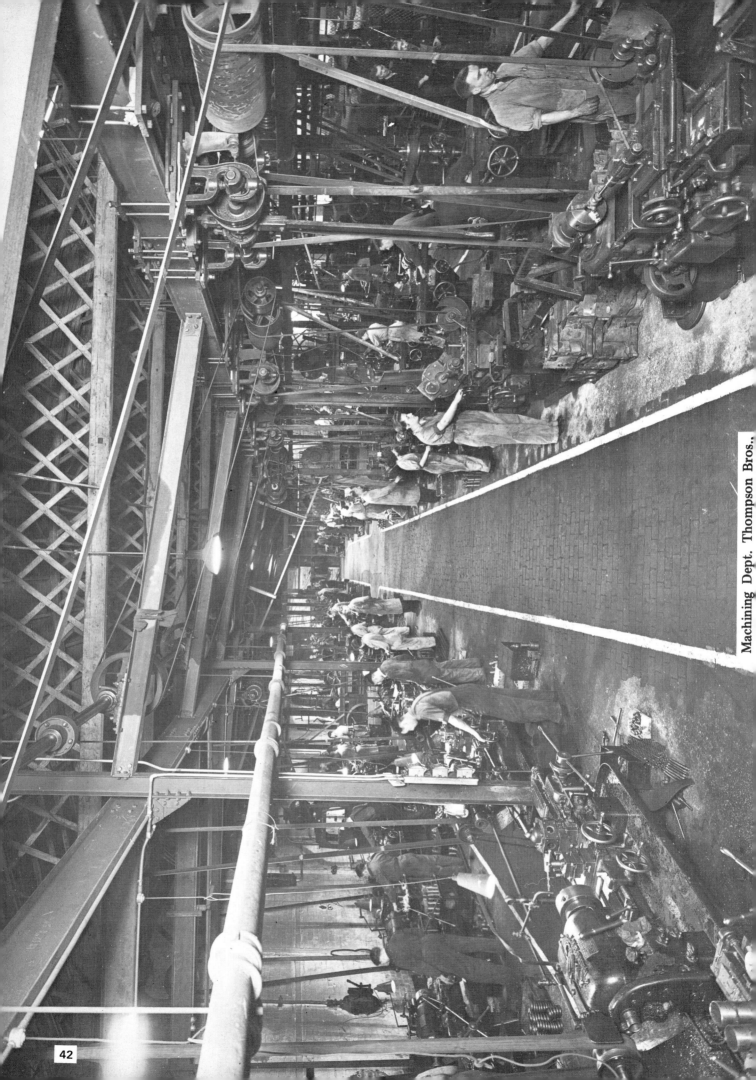

Machining Dept. Thompson Bros..

200 - gallon water tankers, showing purification attachments, nearing completion at Thompson Bros., Bilston.

The Duke of Gloucester visits Goodyear, 7th March 1943.

The "Tube-Roomers", Goodyear, Wolverhampton, September, 1943.

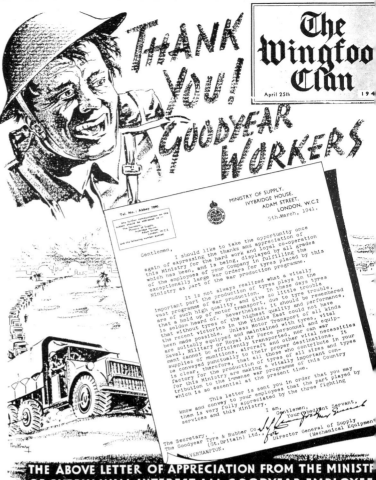

THANK YOU! GOODYEAR WORKERS

The Wingfoot Clan
April 25th 194

MINISTRY OF SUPPLY,
IVYBRIDGE HOUSE,
ADAM STREET,
LONDON, W.C.2
5th March, 1941.

Gentlemen,

I should like to take the opportunity once again of expressing the thanks and appreciation of this Ministry for the hard work and loyal co-operation which has been, and is being, displayed by all grades of the employees of your Company in fulfilling the exceptionally large War Orders for tyres placed by this Ministry as part of the War production programme.

It is not always realized what a vitally important part the production of tyres plays in the vast programme of War production. In these days tyres are of such high quality, and give so little trouble, that a hold up of motor transport, due to tyre trouble, is seldom heard of. Nevertheless, it should be remembered that without tyres of the highest quality and performance, the recent victories in the Middle East would not have been made possible. Unless the Motor Transport of all kinds are suitably equipped and maintained with tyres, vital Naval, Military or Royal Air Force personnel, and equipment cannot be efficiently transported, nor can war supplies of munitions, aircraft and other vital necessities be conveyed punctually to their proper destinations, in your factory for the production of tyres of all sizes and types is clear, therefore, that all those who contribute to the factory for the production of tyres of a vitally important contribution to the immense war programme of this Country which is so essential at the present time.

This letter is sent you in order that you may know and convey to your employees that the part played by them is very fully appreciated by the three fighting services and this Ministry.

I am, Gentlemen,
Your obedient Servant,

for Director General of Supply
(Mechanical Equipment)

The Secretary,
The Goodyear Tyre & Rubber Co (Gt. Britain) Ltd.,
WOLVERHAMPTON.

THE ABOVE LETTER OF APPRECIATION FROM THE MINISTRY OF SUPPLY WILL INTEREST ALL GOODYEAR EMPLOYEES

A floating jetty for Mulberry.

Naval multiple Bofors gun.

One of the mobile power stations for

Landing Craft used on D-Day. The men who built it at John Thompson Ltd., and the girls who launched it.

Eileen Kirkham of Church Lane, Stonnall, Walsall, believed to be the first girl to work in an LMS signal-box, 25th May 1942. ▷

As rail-gangers were soon joining the Forces, it became commonplace to see women take their places laying rails and generally keeping the permanent way in good condition for the conveyance of raw materials, finished war weapons and troops. 20th December 1943. ▷

This question of Stockings

The stockings part of your wardrobe can hardly be quite the joyous thing it used to be! Nevertheless, a stocking bearing the name Kayser-Bondor is your absolute guarantee that you are getting the very finest which to-day can provide. None of the Kayser-Bondor magic of manufacture is lacking . . . to-day there is no better stocking.

But, the time will surely come when *you will* be able to revel once more in the silken luxury which made the names of Kayser and Bondor so famous among chic and glamorous women. That is certainly something to look forward to . . . . !"

"SOMETHING TO LOOK FORWARD TO . . ."

Two of Walsall Corporation's women plumbers who were trained at the local Technical College to take the places of men called up for the Forces. They graduated from doing minor repairs to eventually completing major repair jobs, 5th May 1943.

"Some Codsall stables converted into a war factory" and work paid at 'piece rates". A Bilston firm co-operating in the project with the Codsall War Industries Committee, 2nd February 1942.

Four blind girls involved in war work at Villiers Engineering Co., Wolverhampton, 28th October 1942.

Step on it!

Dig Now — Don't Delay — Get your garden ready to grow your own vegetables — especially the kinds you can store. Apply to your local Council for an allotment and dig with all your might. Vegetables will be scarcer. Victory may well be won by the country with the most food. It is up to every man and woman to step on it now and make every garden a VICTORY GARDEN.

Thursday, June 13, 1940

HELP WIN THE WAR ON THE KITCHEN FRONT

MINISTRY OF FOOD

June, 1940

BULLETIN

Salads are coming into Season.

Lettuces are already in good supply, and radishes and spring onions to give variety. Eat plenty of salads. They are a secret of good health—and are home grown.

THE MINISTER OF FOOD

ABOVE ALL AVOID WASTE AND SO SAVE SHIPPING

FOOD FACTS

100

The Radio Doctor says:— "If possible gather your green vegetables fresh, cook them and eat them as soon as they are ready. Use the vegetable water for soup. Lettuce isn't the only salad vegetable, and it is by no means the best. Ring the changes on endive, watercress, finely shredded carrot, cabbage, spinach, and raw beetroot."

Today "Food Facts" rea its century ! For nearly two y this feature has helped you to s your wartime cooking problems

Do you remember the recipes potato pastry, wartime champ, p roly ? Or the hints on making a box, bottling fruit without su drying herbs ? These are just a fe the hints and recipes which appeared. `Many equally practical economical are still to come.

Thousands of housewives tell us they cut out " Food Facts " for refere We cannot supply back numbers, so will be wise to start cutting out and keep " Food Facts " with this issue.

RECIPE of the WEEK No. 8

"POTATO JANE"

Time : Preparation 5 minutes. Cooking 45 minutes to an hour. *Ingredients :* 1¼ lb. potatoes, 3 oz. cheese, 2 oz. breadcrumbs, ¼ chopped leek, ¼–½ pint of milk, salt and pepper. *Quantity :* 4 helpings. *Method :* Put a layer of sliced potatoes in a fireproof dish. Sprinkle with some of the leek, crumbs, cheese and seasoning. Fill dish with alternate layers, finishing with a layer of cheese and crumbs. Pour over the milk and bake in a moderate oven for 45 minutes, or steam in a basin for 1 hour. Serve with a raw vegetable salad.

Cheer up end-of-season potatoes. Boil peeled potatoes in fast boiling salted water with a teaspoonful of vinegar. Mash, and cover with chopped parsley and mint or chopped watercress, or chopped carrot tops, or beat in raw chopped spinach, or vegetable or meat extract, or sprinkle with toasted oatmeal or browned crumbs.

Cook large potatoes in their skins in boiling salted water. When they show signs of cracking, add cup of cold water; this will drive heat to the centre of the potato and hasten cooking.

LET US REMIND YO

COOKING GREEN VEGETABLES

If you have a garden, don't cut vegetables until you actually need th

It is a mistake to soak green vegeta for a long time before cooking, as wastes valuable mineral salts. Wash t thoroughly in cold, salted water.

Green vegetables must be cooke quickly as possible. So shred them — is, slice them with a knife. Shred green vegetable except spinach, w cooks so quickly it does not nee Divide cauliflowers into sprigs.

Green vegetables should never drowned in water. You need only enough water to keep your pan from b ing — usually a teacupful will do.

Bring the water to the boil, add a salt, and put in the shredded greens.

Now put the lid on the pan. Th important because the greens are t " steamed boiled," and if the st escapes the pan may go dry.

Cook steadily for about 10 to 15 min Give the pan a shake or two during time. Serve at once.

FOOD FACTS No. 100. THE MINISTRY OF FOOD, LONDON,

Troops helping on the land, September, 1941.

A "Grow More Food" campaign at Barnford Hill Park, Langley Green, 9th March 1940.

A "Dig for Victory" exhibition held in Smethwick Baths, December, 1940.

Will you please help to "Feed the Pigs"

Dearly beloved brethren, is it not a sin,
When ye peel potatoes, to throw away the skin,
The skins feed the pigs, and the pigs feed we,
Dearly beloved brethren, what think ye?
AN OLD DEVONSHIRE RHYME.

Are you saving all *your* kitchen waste such as potato or other vegetable peelings, outside cabbage leaves, pea and bean pods, bacon rinds, etc., in fact any " scraps " which cannot be used in your own household ? Do not throw them in with your ashes. The pigs need them and every bit you can save is a help to the National Food Effort.

When you have saved them be sure that they are properly utilized. See that your local authorities organize efficient collection and disposal to pig or poultry keepers. If you live in a village or in the country where no collection is possible organize a local pig club.

Awbridge Farm, Trysull where a good corn harvest is being gathered.

This appeal is inserted by **Whiteways Cyder Co. Ltd.**, who have regularly fed kitchen waste to their herd of over a thousand pigs kept in their Cyder apple orchards. Their Managing Director, Mr. Ronald Whiteway, J.P., of Whimple, Devon, is Chairman of the Kitchen Waste Sub-Committee of the Devon County War Agricultural Committee and will be pleased to answer any questions from householders, local authorities or pig keepers.

To increase home production of food, the Government set up a Ploughing-Up Scheme. Here, in November 1939, the farmer's family help to grub out an old hedge to produce more arable land.

Park Farm, Coven, 11th September 1942. Machines that reap and thresh in one operation are speedily getting in the harvest.

ows That Give Most Milk Will Get Biggest Ration

Daily Mail Agricultural Correspondent

cows that give most ilk will get the biggest when rationing of feed- uffs for farm animals comes into force on February 1. The ration for dairy cows will be 3lb. of feed a day, plus 3½lb. for each gallon of milk in excess of a gallon and a half per day per cow. Goats will receive 1lb. a day, plus 14lb. for each 4 gallons of milk in excess of 4 pints per goat in milk. For other cattle, horses, and sheep, Ministry of Agriculture experts have based rations on numbers on each holding. The farm horse will get 9lb. a day; other horses 2lb., and stallions 5½lb. Farmers will be given coupons. Small poultry keepers with up to 50 birds will have ration cards. Pig and poultry keepers will be allowed one-third of the quantities needed to maintain their pre-war pigs and poultry. I understand the foodstuffs have been dispersed all over the country to avoid the local shortages that occurred last winter.

FARMER'S BOY

The National Farmer's Union asks for Government control to continue after the war.

Members of the Haddock Road, Bilston Pig Club cast an appraising eye at their six porkers. The members built the piggery themselves in their spare time, 22nd May 1942.

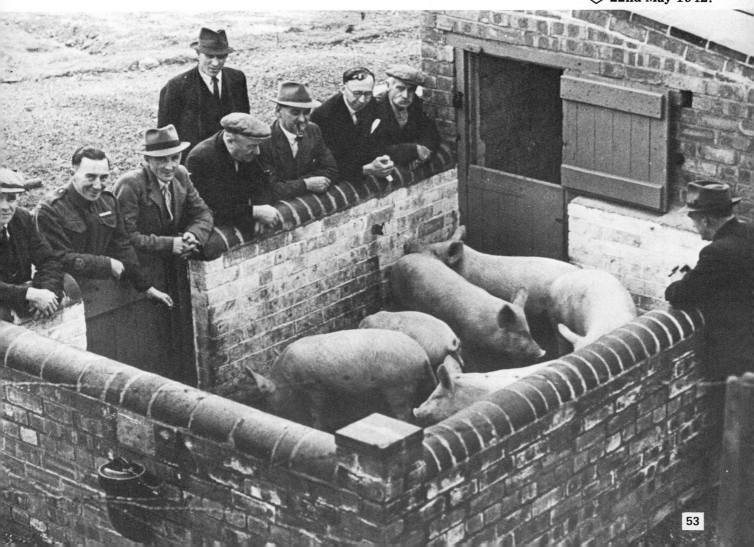

ENTERTAINMENT AND SPORT

The daily papers for Monday, 4th September 1939, carried along with reports of Britain's first day at war, the news that public places of entertainment were closed, and all sporting events where crowds were liable to gather including athletics, greyhound racing, football, cricket, speedway racing and boxing, were cancelled until further notice for fear of heavy casualties from air-raids.

On Saturday, 2nd September, 370,000 fans had watched league football games despite travelling difficulties. Spurs arrived at West Bromwich with only minutes to spare before the kick-off but managed to score twice early on in the game. Cecil Shaw, Albion's left back, walked off dejectedly at full time having missed a penalty. As he went down the players' tunnel he was told that his wife was about to give birth and it is said that he smiled for the first time all afternoon. There was an incident at Blackpool when a whiskey bottle was thrown at the Wolves goalkeeper. Order was restored when the referee asked two policemen to patrol the crowd. In Walsall's last peacetime game, they scored the only goal of the match in a home win against Queens Park Rangers.

Many amateur football matches were cancelled through players being called up or being on ARP duties. Stewards of the Jockey Club and the National Hunt Committee were expected to meet within a few days to make a decision regarding the future of racing. However, no immediate decision was taken on the Ryder Cup golf tournament in which Britain was due to play America in Jacksonville, Florida, in November.

Within a few weeks, in response to the lack of bombing and for public morale, the total ban was lifted, though at one time the nearest cinema to the Black Country that could be guaranteed to be open was at Aberystwyth. As cinemas and theatres re-opened timetable changes were enforced because of the possibility of air-raids, and petrol rationing, which meant that there were few buses around after 9.00 p.m.

Football, a massive crowd puller in the 1930's, was organised on a regional basis with the Albion, Wolves and Walsall finding themselves in League South. On 1st November 1940 the Albion met a Czech army side which included the internationals Michna, Keike and Vocasek. Albion, in good form, having recently beaten Swansea 8 - 2, were third in the league, with Walsall 6th and Wolves 11th, though the latter improved to win the 1941/42 League (War) Cup.

Horse racing continued. On 30th May 1940 the first three horses past the Park Hurdle Plate were all disqualified for going round the wrong course, the race being awarded to "Another Consul". Gordon Richards was still undecided about his mount for the "New Derby".

Cricket survived even though the Oval was converted into a prisoner-of-war camp, then not used.

The embryonic BBC television service closed for the duration of the war but few people in 1939 had sets anyway. However, nine out of ten homes did have a radio and it was the re-organised Home Service that produced some memorable programmes, including "ITMA", "Band Waggon", "Workers' Playtime" and "Hi Gang".

THE SONG BIRD OF THE SCREEN IN HER FIRST TECHNICOLOR TRIUMPH . . .

DEANNA DURBIN
ROBERT PAIGE
AKIM TAMIROFF
in

"CAN'T HELP SINGING"

The REAL BEAUTY of DEANNA DURBIN SHOWN AT LAST IN TECHNICOLOR

⇧ Kenneth More developed his talents at The Grand, Wolverhampton, before joining the Royal Navy.

⇧ Frequent visitors to the Black Country, Eric Morecambe and Ernie Wise.

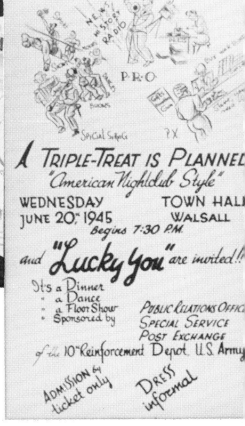

Three girl workers join with an ENSA concert party in leading community singing at a factory lunch-time concert.

The Terry "Toby Jug" Cantor ENSA Concert Party. Mr. Cantor wears the trilby.

BING CROSBY TOP

Bing Crosby, Gary Cooper, and Bob Hope, in that order, were the three most popular stars of 1944 according to a "Motion Picture Herald" poll, quoted in a Hollywood message.

Crosby was fourth last year, but "Going My Way?" put him at the top for this year.

Stourbridge Cricket Club, 1940.

The ALBION NEWS
and OFFICIAL PROGRAMME

Vol. XXXVI (New Series).   No. 1 (Copyright)   AUGUST 7th, 1944.

WEST BROMWICH ALBION FOOTBALL CLUB, LIMITED

Directors: Mr. L. J. Nurse (Chairman), Major H. Wilson Keys, M.C., T.D. (Vice-Chairman), Mr. A. Claude Jephcott, Councillor N. W. Bassett, Major W. H. Thursfield and Mr. W. E. Jephcott.
Secretary : Mr. Fred Everiss, J.P.   Ground : The Hawthorns, West Bromwich.
Telegraphic Address: "Football, West Bromwich."   Telephone No.: 0005 West Bromwich
Club Colours : Shirts—Navy Blue and White Stripes.   Knickers—White.
(All communications regarding editorial matter in this programme should be addressed to The Editor, The Albion News, The Hawthorns, West Bromwich. For advertisement rates and spaces apply to the Secretary of the Club.)

BASEBALL
AMERICAN ARMY v. CANADIAN ARMY
In aid of the Red Cross Prisoners of War Fund and the Mayor's Comforts Fund.

WELCOME AND THANKS
We welcome our friends from America and Canada to-day to give us our first Baseball game at The Hawthorns in aid of Charity, and we are indebted in particular to Colonel James A. Killian of the U.S. Army for his kindly assistance not only with regard to the game, but also for the splendid U.S.A. Army Drum and Pipe Band which will be in attendance, and to Colonel M. B. Kenner, of the Royal Canadian Medical Corps for his help with the lads of Canada.

Our thanks are also due to His Worship the Mayor, Councillor G. E. Powell, J.P., for his kindly interest and he will be present this afternoon to be introduced to both teams. Also to the Committee who have carried out the work with His Worship the Mayor as chairman. They are : Councillor Norman W. Bassett, Mr. Reg. Boardman, Mr. E. Houghton Harris and Mr. Fred Everiss (hon. secretary). We trust the results will be all they would desire.

BASEBALL THE AMERICAN WAY
FOLLOW THE GAME
A match consists of nine innings for each team, but a game can count if terminated by the Umpire after five innings. An innings terminates when three men of the batting side are out. The distribution of the fielding side is as follows: 1, Pitcher ; 2, Catcher ; 3, 1st Base ; 4, 2nd Base ; 5, 3rd Base ; 6, Short Stop ; 7, Left Fielder ; 8, Centre Fielder ; 9, Right Fielder.

NOTE :—When Pitcher is delivering the ball to bat he must keep one foot in contact with the Pitcher's Plate. Pitching distance is 60 feet, 6 inches.

The batsman is allowed three strikes, or four balls. A strike is a ball which passes over the home plate between the knee and shoulder of batter, or any ball struck at by the batsman without touching the bat. A ball is called when the pitched ball is below the knee or above the shoulder, or which passes wide of the home plate. If pitcher sends down four balls before three strikes, batsman is allowed first base. Batsman becomes a base runner when a fair hit is made or when he gets first base on balls. A fair hit is one which settles or flies over fair ground, that is inside the foul lines (see diagram). A baserunner is out at first base if ball is held on bag before he reaches it. At second, third, and home plate baserunner must be touched by ball which is held by a fielder before he reaches the bases, except when play is forced, that is when base runners are compelled to advance through batsman making a fair hit and becoming a runner, when all that is necessary is for a fielder to hold a ball and touch the base. The ball is dead and not in play if it goes foul, that is, outside the foul lines (see diagram), unless it is caught, batsman is then declared out. A run is scored only when each individual batsman has made a complete circuit of the course touching each base in regular order before three men are out.

THE DIAMOND

Left Fielder   Centre Fielder   Right Fielder
(Short Stop)   2nd Baseman

Pitcher's Box
Batsman — Catcher

Distance between bases is 60 feet.
Pitching Distance 60 feet 6 inches

---

8. In consideration of the observance by the said player of the terms, provisions and conditions of this Agreement, the said *Frank C. Buckley* ....on behalf of the Club hereby agrees that the said Club shall pay to the said Player the sum of £ *6-0-0* per week from *8 MAY 1939* to *26 AUG 1939* and £ *7-0-0* per week from *27 AUG 1939* to *4 MAY 1940*.

9. This Agreement (subject to the Rules of The Football Association) shall cease and determine on *4 MAY 1940* unless the same shall have been previously determined in accordance with the provisions hereinbefore set forth.

Fill in any other provisions required.

The Player to be paid extra per week when playing in Reserve Team £

,, ,, ,, First Team £ *1-0-0*

If at any time during the period of this Agreement the wages herein agreed to be paid shall be in excess of the wages permitted to be paid by the Club to the player in accordance with the Rules of the Football League, the wages to be paid to the player shall be the amount the Club is entitled to pay by League Rules in force from time to time, and this Agreement shall be read and construed as if it were varied accordingly.

As Witness the hands of the said parties the day and year first aforesaid

Signed by the said.... *Frank C. Buckley* ....

....................and

....*Joseph Gardiner.*....

In the presence of

(Signature) .... *J. Howley* ....

(Occupation) ....*Ass. Sec. Wolves.*....

(Address) ....*229, Park Lane,*....

....*Wolverhampton.*....

J. Gardiner (Player).

Frank C. Buckley (Secretary).

West Bromwich Albion F.C. 1939

Wolverhampton Wanderers, 1939.

Walsall Town F.C. 1939.
Bert Williams, who provided this photograph, is 4th from left in the second row down.

THE BOMBING

By the summer of 1939, Europe was heading inexorably towards war and the military planners of both sides set to work.

In June the Luftwaffe began a major reconnaissance of the United Kingdom, priority being given to industrial and communications targets. Thousands of factories, mines, chemical plants, refineries, railway yards, bridges, power stations, water and sewerage works and so on were individually identified and plotted on pirated copies of Ordanance Survey Maps.

By the end of October 1940 the Luftwaffe were not having things entirely their own way. The blitz on London was being waged at a high cost in men and machines, and there was no sign of a British surrender, or a willingness to discuss an armistice, only a stiffening of resolve. Within a few weeks of commencing their attack on London, the Luftwaffe had no more than 700 serviceable bombers left. New aircraft were getting to the front line squadrons, but badly needed spares were taking weeks to come through because the bulk of Germany's aircraft industry was still working peace time shifts so as not to undermine public morale!

However, by the beginning of November, the situation had deteriorated so much that Göring was forced to call off large scale daylight attacks and issue a new directive. London was to remain the main target but the Luftwaffe would now turn its attention to the industrial areas of Britain. Coventry, Birmingham and Wolverhampton were among the places named to be attacked at night using the X-Gërat radio navigational aid.

With the exception of a few specialized units, the Luftwaffe had done virtually nothing to train its bomber crews for night operations. There had been no need. Their operations against Poland, Denmark, Norway, Belguim, Holland and France had, for the most part, been carried out in daylight and in support of ground and/or naval forces. The air war against Britain was different.

One special unit was Kampfgruppe 100 (KGr100) who were to play an important role in pioneering pathfinder techniques and rank equal with similar Allied formations. KGr100's aircraft were equipped with X-Gërat, a radio navigational system that worked with the aid of ground transmitters to guide the aircraft to the target and automatically relieve the bomb load. Another target-finding device was Knickebein. This worked with only two transmitters and had a greater range than X-Gërat but was less accurate and prone to the electronic counter measures of the RAF's No. 80 Wing.

Beginning around the 29th October 1940, Luftwaffe photo-reconnaissance planes made a series of passes over Coventry, Birmingham and Wolverhampton to assess likely target areas, and what anti-aircraft defences, if any, were in place.

On the 11th November, the Government Code & Cypher School at Bletchley succeeded in decoding a German signal transmitted on the 9th to KGr100 laying down signal procedures for an operation code named "Moonlight Sonata". The operation was to be something special, for a call-sign was allocated to none other than Göring himself. The Commander-in-Chief was taking a personal interest. The target was not indentified. Various codenames were mentioned including "Korn" and Target 1, 2, 3 and 4. One lead however was that KGr100 was to transmit a calibration signal at 1300 hours on the day of the attack, which was to be repeated by Air Fleets 2 and 3.

On the 12th, Air Intelligence received a decrypt of a message transmitted by KGr100 listing target 51 "Einheitpreis", target 52 "Regenschirm" and target 53 "Korn" but not mentioning "Operation Moonlight Sonata".

The same day a captured German pilot was overheard telling his cellmate that a massive attack was planned to take place between 15 - 20th November and that Coventry and Birmingham were the targets.

On the evening of the 13th, the captured pilot mentioned "Regenschirm" which means umbrella, pointing to Birmingham, the home of Neville Chamberlain, the umbrella man. Einheitpreis' was translated to "all-at-one-price" meaning Woolworths which suggested Wolverhampton. "Korn", on the other hand, could not be positively identified.

In the early hours of the 14th, the RAF drew up a counter plan codenamed 'Operation Cold Water" and Fighter Command's few night-fighter squadrons were dispersed so as to be able to operate over Greater London or the Midlands.

At 1300 hours on the 14th, KGr100's calibration signal was detected and by 1500 hours No. 80 Wing was convinced that the target was Coventry and the Directorate of Home Operations of the Air Ministry then warned the RAF home commands accordingly.

That night Coventry was attacked by 469 bombers. So devastating was the attack that the government lifted the restriction on the media in naming a bombed town. The image of the city, with a third of its centre destroyed, including its cathedral, appeared in newspapers around the world and aroused strong feelings against Nazi Germany.

Birmingham's date with destiny came on the night of 22nd/23rd November, when during its worst raid to date, three vital water mains were severed, leaving much of the city without water. Fire appliances were stationed round what supplies remained, and, in anticipation of another night's bombing, Royal Engineers were brought in with orders to blow firebreaks wherever necessary — no building was to be considered immune, for the whole city would be in danger if a firestorm was allowed to develop.

Wolverhampton's great raid never materialized. German photo-reconnaissance reports mention a massive increase in anti-aircraft defences, and assumed that the RAF would also be waiting for the incoming bombers. Though Luftwaffe archives are incomplete, it is possible that Wolverhampton may have originally been scheduled to be attacked in force before Coventry, but the raid was postponed. It is interesting to note that Wolverhampton's increased defences, in part, consisted of dummy guns, sited on Penn Common, made from telegraph poles aligned on a typical A/A gun elevation, each flanked by a pair of cartwheels.

Many small raids were spread over the Black Country, though thankfully casualties were light. For example at Darlaston 11 people were killed, 48 injured, 11 houses destroyed and 401 damaged. Aldridge had one fatality, 23 injured, 6 houses detroyed and 355 damaged. Walsall's casualties were 6 killed, 38 injured, 10 houses destroyed and 1967 damaged.

Cottages at Rowley Regis, 22nd November 1940.

Mine damage, S. Smith & Sons, Brewery Street, Smethwick, December, 1940.

Smethwick, 23rd October 1940.

Remains of a German bomber shot down over Smethwick, April, 1941.

⇧
Rear of Holy Trinity Schools, Smethwick after mine damage, December, 1940.

JIM McKENZIE *(Sandwell Councillor)*
"The day that war started we found the Territorials encamped in and around the Drill Hall, in Broomfield, and we earned ourselves quite a lot of pocket money fetching beer for them.

As a 13 year old I remember the tremendous explosion when the fire-bomb hit the gasometer in Rabone Lane (the old Smethwick works). Fortunately there were no other German planes about otherwise Smethwick would have been devastated with so much industry around."

⇦
Gas Dept., High Street, West Bromwich, 19th November 1940. The censor insisted that the car number plates should be obliterated before the photograph could be used.

Walsall Road, Stone Cross, 10th November 1940.

Hallam Hospital Laundry, West Bromwich, 19th November 1940. The censor instructed that the chimney stack must not be shown!

Great Bridge, 16th May 1941.

⌂ Wood Green Cemetery Chapel, Wednesbury.

⌂ The end of the game in Walsall!

Clearing up in Bilston, 21st August 1940.

HARRY RICHARDS *(County Councillor) "I was a youngster in a family of 14 living in Ryle Street, Bloxwich. Over came the German bombers (27th October 1940) and off came the roofs of numbers 31, 33 and 35. The family next door but one to us consisted of 14 and 9 people respectively, so together with our 14 that made 37 altogether who became the very first people in the district to be rendered homeless. It was many, many months before our four bedroomed house was repaired and we could return home.*

On the day of the raid, my mother had already decided that our Anderson shelter in the garden was too damp for us to occupy. The shelter was bombed out of existence that very night!

Our 'incident' was the very first action test for all the emergency services – fire, police, ambulance, ARP control room, evacuation and rehousing section, gas and electricity, etc. It was the considered opinion that they all came through their baptism of fire with a great deal of merit."

The buildings look a sorry mess, but what about the potatoes in the foreground? They have been completely stripped of their foliage by the blast. Wombourne, 9th July 1941.

R. M. Sievwright and Co. Ltd.,
coachbuilders of Cleveland Road,
Wolverhampton, 1942.

⇧ Wood Road, Tettenhall after a lone German bomber's visit. The Nuffield Hospital now occupies this site.

⇩ Carlton Road, Wolverhampton.

Bloomfield Road, Tipton,
19th November, 1940.

Early one bleak, wartime winter evening, two landmines were dropped 40 yards apart in Quarry Bank but failed to explode. Such mines were a vicious weapon and caused massive devastation. 2,000 residents were evacuated (though some folk in streets quite close to the incident were forgotten!). Navy Bomb Disposal squads defused both mines with very little time left before they were due to explode. Such was the relief of the residents of Quarry Bank that the following day the churches and chapels held thanksgiving services. Every place was full to overflowing. Nothing like it had happened before so people came to call the place "The Holy City"!

Bomb crater in Upper
Gornal. 27th June 1940.

Grace Mary Estate, Tividale, November, 1940.

HORACE VANES *"A large bomb, about a 1000 - pounder, landed by the side of "The Cracker" (a quarry in The Old Park, Dudley), but it failed to go off. As I was on stand-by, as part of the mobile unit, I was called out. We cleared the area and all the windows in the houses in Himley Road, Stourbridge Road, Grange Road and Scotts Green had to be opened before it could be detonated!"*

Top Church, Dudley shows its scars after bombs dropped nearby. 5th September 1940.

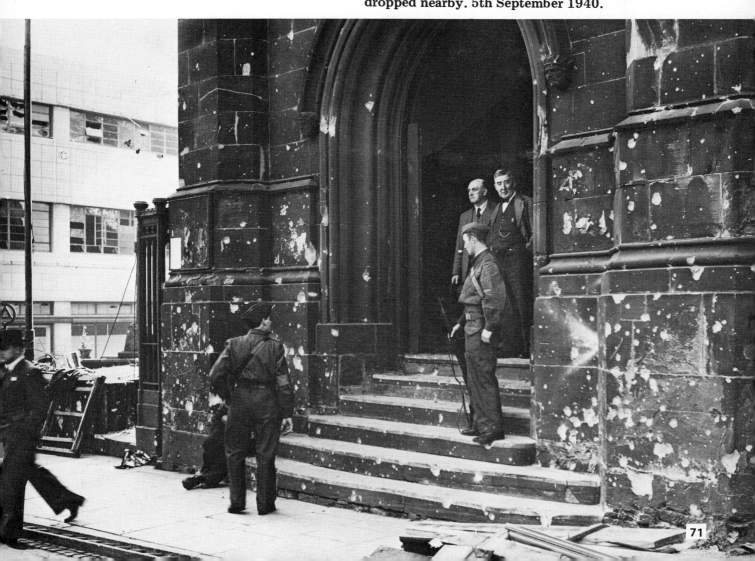

FORM C.2.

File No. 9|5|867

Please quote this file number in all correspondence.

WAR DAMAGE COMMISSION
(Form C.2)

Claim for Temporary Works Payment and Cost of Works Payment under Part I of the War Damage Act, 1941

PROPERTY

12 Wood Street

Woodside

Dudley

Mr. C. J. Rubery,
10 Holly Street,
Holly Hall
Dudley

The War Damage Commissioners learn with regret that you have suffered war damage to your property and direct me to acknowledge receipt of your Notification of Damage (Form C.1). From the particulars given on your form it appears that the claim is likely to be one for a Temporary Works and Cost of Works Payment. This form (C.2) is the one mentioned in Form C.1 on which you are asked to give the more detailed information required by the Commission for the consideration of your claim.

The form is designed to enable you to claim payment for any repairs already done at your expense, and to give notice of any further works necessary to make good the damage to the property. If further repairs are necessary, please advise the War Damage Commission when you are able to have them done. The Commission will then supply you with a form of claim

If any repairs have already been done or if you are now able to have them done you should complete this form and return it within 30 days of the completion of the repairs.

If you have not had any repairs done and are not able to have them done at present you should complete this form with the exception of paragraph (1) and return it as soon as possible.

If it has been found since you completed Form C.1 that the property was damaged beyond repair, will you please return this form and notify the Commission accordingly at the address given below. The appropriate form for a Value Payment will then be sent to you.

F. P. ROBINSON
Secretary

Date 21/11/41

When completed this form should be returned to

WAR DAMAGE COMMISSION
REGIONAL OFFICE
MIDLAND HOSPITAL
EASY ROW
BIRMINGHAM

WARNING.

If the cost of making good the war damage to this property will ultimately exceed £1,000 or ten times the net annual value of the property you are required to furnish the Commission with particulars of the work (other than temporary works) before it is put in hand. (See London Gazette of ....19 AUG 1941....)

German incendiary bomb. ▷

TOMMY MUNDON *("Black Country Night Out" comedian) "My dad worked for the fire service and one night he went to deal with a bomb that had gone through someone's ceiling. The mattress had gone up in smoke and, due to the heat, hundreds of feathers stuck to dad. I was 5 at the time and when he walked into our house in Chapel Street, Halesowen, he looked just like a large turkey."*

A bomb disposal team tackle a 1,000 Kg. device. ▷

Bomb-proof shelter at Marsh & Baxter's, Brierley Hill, built to house 1,500 people.

FIRE

Formed during the late 1930's to reinforce the regular brigades in times of emergency, the Auxilliary Fire Service (AFS) was to play an important role during the early years of war. Equipment consisted of trailer pumps and an assortment of vehicles converted from civilian use, though some specially designed fire engines did exist.

On 13th May 1941, Home Secretary Herbert Morrison announced his nationalisation plan to Parliament and within a week the Fire Service (Emergency Provisions) Bill, 1941, became law. On 18th August all independent brigades ceased to exist and were incorporated into the National Fire Service (NFS), the majority of Black Country units being assigned to either No. 24 or No. 40 Fire Forces.

It should not be overlooked that women played an important role in the AFS, not only on the administration side, but as front line fire-fighters.

△ NFS Fire Force 40 (Kinver) are inspected by the Regional Commander, the Earl of Dudley, 5th May 1943.

Issued by the Fire Offices' Committee as part of a National Campaign supported by Government Departments concerned

Bobbington Fire Party.

No. 335

County Borough of Wolverhampton.

Air Raid Precautions Organisation.

Auxiliary Fire Service.

This is to certify that

Fredk. M. Woollaston

has completed a course of training under the auspices of the County Borough of Wolverhampton Fire Brigade and has qualified by examination to become a member of the Auxiliary Fire Service.

Dated 12 July, 1939.

Chief Constable and
Chief Officer Fire Brigade.

Thompson Bros., AFS.

Smethwick part-time members of the NFS at Rolfe Street, Divisional HQ during a quiz to test the knowledge of members.
The Question-Master (centre) is Assistant Commander Bloom.

Display of fire-fighting equipment outside the Blue Gates, Smethwick.

Coven part-time crew take part in the NFS competition at Tipton.

Wolverhampton AFS demonstration at the local canal side. Note the waterborne fire tender with fire-fighting equipment and pennant.

AFS vehicle and trailer pump designed by Billinghams of Wolverhampton and built by W. Robinson & Co.

A new fire tender, AFS, Tettenhall.

The King & Queen inspect the Women's AFS.

A.F.S.—Auxiliary Fire Service. A specialised job for trained personnel. Driving staff cars and light lorries, and important work in the watch-room and at the switchboard.

Men and Women with **WILLS TO WIN** *are smoking* **GOLD FLAKE**

MADE OF PURE VIRGINIA TOBACCO
BY W. D. & H. O. WILLS

Women's AFS, West Bromwich, 1940.

NFS Officers and Firewomen risk taking a few moments off to pose at Dudley Fire Station (Z1) in Tower Street,

symbolise the fighting spirit of the Black Country.

THE HOME GUARD

"Operation Dynamo" was a success. It is 4th June 1940 and the evacuation of British and Allied troops from the Continent via Dunkirk is complete. Altogether 336,427 men are safely landed at ports in England, devoid, in most cases, of their weapons, desperately tired and some nursing wounds badly needing medical attention.

Winston Churchill, the Prime Minister, addressing Parliament on that day, asked that the deliverance be not hailed as a victory. "Wars are not won by evacuations," he said.

The fight against Nazi Germany was to continue, Britain alone now that her Continental Allies were defeated. And, remember, America had not yet entered the war.

How, then, to defend the British Isles?

We had a home-based Navy; we had a growing number of airfields and landing grounds to accommodate the RAF; and now we had drawn in our badly mauled troops from the Continent to supplement our domestic Army.

On the minds of everyone in these islands was the one word: INVASION.

British and Allied regular forces must needs be released from all other duties except:

1) the coastal watch and coastal batteries;
2) the making of landward defences;
3) support troops in immediate support of the above two;
4) mobile columns and brigade groups;

and

5) the General Reserve.

Did we have sufficient troops for all these duties? Perhaps not.

The Rt. Hon. Anthony Eden, Minister of State for War, planned the raising of Local Defence Volunteers (LDV) to augment the regular troops; he broadcast an immediate appeal for civilian men between the ages of 17 and 65 to report, without delay, to their local Police Stations for vetting (to weed out potential Fifth Columists), although no medical examination was required.

Anthony Eden:

"Now is your opportunity. We want large numbers of men in Great Britain who are British subjects between the ages of 17 and 65 to come forward now and offer their services in order to make assurance doubly sure. You will not be paid but you will receive uniforms and will be armed."

Men surged forward in their tens of thousands: those under age "advanced" a year or two and those over age shed a few "annual rings".

The first LDV's were provided with a stencilled arm-band, a whistle and a pike-shaft or broom-handle. It was not until after August, 1940 that uniforms were supplied and Churchill, having his own way, renamed this civilian army The Home Guard.

American ships arrived at our ports, under early "Lend-Lease" arrangements, bearing precious cargoes of rifles. The Home Guard in every county, every town and every village sat up all night to receive them; men and women toiled day and night making them fit for use. Now the Home Guard could possess .300 rifles, allowing the transfer of 30,000 British type rifles to the rapidly expanding Regular Army.

Winston Churchill:

"We shall not falter nor fail. We shall go on to the end. We shall defend our island whatever the cost may be. We shall fight on the beaches, the landing grounds, in the fields, in the streets and on the hills."

By May, 1941 some 1,600,000 volunteers had enrolled, and more important, were adequately armed.

Gradually more sophisticated weapons came along:— sten guns, sticky-bombs, Blacker Bombards, Northover Projectors and the Browning Automatic Rifle. (The latter brought new words like sear, rear-sear, rear-sear-retainer and rear-sear-retainer-keeper to the vocabulary of the Home Guardsmen!)

Churchill urged the Home Guard be allowed to man light anti-aircraft guns and heavy searchlights. At last the "Look, Duck and Vanish" image of the earlier cynics faded. The Home Guard had come of age.

Platoons formed Companies and Companies formed Battalions; this was the Regular Army structure. Army ranks and badges were matched by Army discipline.

There were sad moments and humorous ones: A Fordhouses platoon, helping to defend Pendeford aerodrome and the Boulton Paul Aircraft factory, manned a road-block in Wobaston Road. As dusk fell, a cyclist zig-zagged his way through the hazards. Twice the cry of 'Halt! Who goes there?" rang out. No response. A third and final challenge -- still the cyclist pedalled on. A shot rang out; the cyclist received fatal wounds. Only later was it discovered that he was deaf.

Robert Louch, patrolling near the factory as a member of the (then) Thompson Bros. Home Guard Company, Bilston, was more than startled one misty night by a white shape that moved silently to and fro. Dutifully he reported on the field telephone "I can see a ghost! Shall I shoot it?" The guard commander sent reinforcements and the ghost was cornered, not without a little apprehension. The spectre turned out to be a local gypsy's horse, and because it was piebald only its irregular white portions showed up in the dark, giving the impression of a ghostly presence!

Another guardsman, having imbibed rather well before duty, was quite suddenly missed by his fellow patroller. A a quiet hail or two brought a cry from the canal: "Here I am up to me flamin' arm-pits in the cut!" It took the remainder of their off-duty time to dry out his uniform, his field-dressings, his tin of anti-gas ointment and to trick out his rifle in a manner fit for the dismissal parade in the early hours of the next day. Many a Black Country factory, naturally having a convenient rail-link, used the railway lines to mount mobile anti-aircraft guns. It was frequently reported that the Home Guardsmen, patrolling those same railway lines, were often in as much danger from shrapnel from our own guns as they were from enemy bombs. In Wednesbury, the tin-hat was said to have been literally a life-saver when some particularly heavy and jagged shrapnel thumped down during one raid.

All training, particularly in the handling of weapons, was taken seriously and real danger was never far away. The Molotov Cocktail (a combination of petrol and a wick contained in a glass bottle) was most hazardous to handle during the early days of tuition.

The Blacker Bombard often failed to explode and, if a Home Guardsman was placed to protect the missile (from whom?!) then a ten minute stint could seem like twenty-four hours. In the event, the Regular Army instructor was known to pick up the lethal projectile and to toss it casually into his small truck before driving off!

Marksmanship was paramount so, to encourage high skills, a National Savings Certificate worth at that time 15 shillings (75 new pence) was a typical, patriotic prize awarded to the owner of the best shooting-card handed in from the rifle range.

On 7th September, 1940, much movement of enemy barges and small ships was detected by British Intelligence. Four Germans, captured a few days earlier after landing from a rowing-boat on our south coast, confessed to being spies. They had been briefed to report on British troop movement in the Ipswich-London-Reading-Oxford area during the favourable moon and tide conditions which would prevail between 8th and 10th September.

The Chiefs of Staff therefore considered that invasion possibilities were high and sent the code-word "Cromwell" — invasion imminent.

At 8.00 p.m. the signal went out and, all over the country Home Guard commanders, acting on their own initiative, called out the Home Guard by ringing the church bells. Rumours abounded. As a result of this false alarm it was decided that church bells be rung only by an order from a Home Guard who had seen 25 or more parachutists landing. No mention of this incident was made in the newspapers or in Parliament, but it had served as a useful tonic and rehearsal for all concerned.

Late in 1944 the Home Guard, tried and found true, battered in many cases by enemy air-raids, was finally 'stood-down''. Note that phrase. It was not disbanded; the men were not demobilised. Are they therefore, technically, still serving?

Those who served in the Home Guard were entitled to the Defence Medal.

"History will say that your share in the greatest of all our struggles for freedom was a vitally important one. You have given your service without thought of reward. You have earned in full measure your country's gratitude."

(H.M. King George VI., Colonel-in-Chief.)

Home Guard All-Night Exercise, Cannock ⬆
Chase, 1941.

The Duke of Kent inspects the Home Guard in
Dudley Market Place, 19th December 1940. ⬇

"D" Coy 39th Staffs. (Enville) Bn, Home Guard at rear of White Harte Hotel Kinver, October, 1941.

Battalion Home Guard

What you MUST do when the Home Guard is mustered.

1.—Put on uniform with great coat, and take the whole of your equipment to the place where you have been instructed to report.

2.—Bring the undermentioned articles with you:—

   (a) Enough food to last 24-hrs. drinking mug and plate or mess tin, with knife, fork and spoon, and water.

   (b) Razor, lather brush, handbrush and comb, towel, soap, toilet paper.

   (c) Change of underclothing, spare pair of socks, handkerchiefs. (Have a sand-bag ready to hold the above, with your Name, No. and Platoon plainly marked on it).

   (d) One blanket, rolled bandolier fashion.

   (e) Identity Card.

   (f) All your ration books.

3.—Keep this part of the form in the breast pocket of Battle Dress.

4.—Fill in the following details (in ink) and hand slip to your Platoon Officer when reporting for duty on mustering.

- -

NOT TO BE DETACHED UNTIL MUSTERED.

Nat. Reg. No. *OQPK 35/1*

NAME *EVERALL C.*
(Block Letters).

ADDRESS *430 PENN ROAD WOLVERHAMPTON*

Rank *LIEUT.*   Bn. No. *22*

Company *2 C/A*   Platoon *5*

TO BE HANDED OVER TO PLATOON OFFICER ON REPORTING FOR DUTY WHEN MUSTERED.

Date .... Time of Reporting ....

A.F.W 4026.

Certificate of Proficiency
HOME GUARD

On arrival at the Training Establishment, Primary Training Centre or Recruit Training Centre, the holder must produce this Certificate at once for the officer commanding, together with Certificate A if gained in the Junior Training Corps or Army Cadet Force.

PART I. I hereby certify that (Rank) *Pte* (Name and initials) *Wilson H.* of *D* ~~Battery~~ Company *84th S.S. Bilston* ~~Regiment~~ Battalion HOME GUARD has qualified in the Proficiency Badge tests as laid down in the pamphlet "Qualifications for, and Conditions governing the Award of the Home Guard Proficiency Badges and Certificates" for the following subjects :

Subject	Date	Initials
1. General knowledge (all candidates)	15·8·43	
2. Rifle	29·8·43	
3. 36 M Grenade	29·8·43	
*4. (a) Other weapon *Blacker Bombard*	August 15	
(b) Signalling		
*5. (a) Battlecraft, (b) Coast Artillery, (c) Heavy A.A. Bty. work, (d) "Z" A.A. Battery work, e) Bomb Disposal (f) Watermanship, (g) M.T.	28·8·43	
*6. (a) Map Reading, (b) Field works, (c) First Aid	15·8·43	

Date *15 AUG 1943* 194—   Signature .... Major

Date .... 194—   Signature .... Major

Date .... 194—   Signature ....

Date .... 194—   Signature ....

Date .... 194—   Signature ....

PART II. I certify that (Rank) *Pte* (Name and initials) *Wilson H.* of *D* ~~Battery~~ Company *84th (BILSTON)* Bn. Staff ~~Regiment~~ Battalion HOME GUARD, having duly passed the Proficiency tests in the subjects detailed above in accordance with the pamphlet and is hereby authorized to wear the Proficiency Badge as laid down in Regulations for the Home Guard, Vol. 1, 1942, para. 41d.

Date .... 194—   Signature .... 84th (BILSTON) Bn. Staffs. H.G.

PART III. If the holder joins H.M. Forces, his Company or equivalent Commander will record below any particulars which he considers useful in assessing the man's value on arrival at the T.E., P.T.C., R.T.C., e.g. service, rank, duties on which employed, power of leadership, etc.

Pte. H. Wilson, OSGB 15/5 has given 1 year 9 months of most excellent service in this Company of the Home Guard.
He is a good Rifle Shot and has had special training as a Sharpshooter.
He has also proved himself to be a most capable member of a 29 m/m. Spigot Mortar Team.
I can thoroughly and confidently recommend him.

Date .... 194—   Signature ....
COMPANY COMMANDER, "D" COMPANY,
84th (BILSTON) BATTALION,
STAFFORDSHIRE HOME GUARD.

"D" Coy, Accles & Pollock Home Guard,
Paddock Works, Oldbury.

Parade of Home Guard at Cape Hill Brewery, Smethwick, 1940.

"D" Coy 20th Bn. Worcs. Regt. at Grange Park.

"D" Coy, (Thompson Bros. Unit) 34th (Bilston) Bn. South Staffs Home Guard.

'C' Coy 22nd Bn. Home Guard stand-down Bradmore, 1944.

Colonel Up and Private Down *by Walter*

'A' Coy 20th Staffs. (Wolverhampton) Home Guard, July 1944 at Courtaulds, Jackson Street, Witmore Reans. ⇨

In the years when our Country

was in mortal danger

Horace Vanes

who served

gave generously of his time and

powers to make himself ready

for her defence by force of arms

and with his life if need be.

George R.I

THE HOME GUARD

The Laying-up of the Home Guard Colours at Top Church, Dudley.

THE MILITARY

Although Black Country men and women served in numerous branches of the armed forces, the South Staffordshire Regiment is synonymous with the area.

In September 1939, the regiment's regular battalions were on foreign service, the 1st in Palestine and the 2nd in India. Six months earlier the government had announced its plans to expand the Territorial Army, with the result that the 5th (Walsall) battalion was reinforced with a newly formed 7th battalion, and the 6th (Wolverhampton) was re-structured to become the 1/6th and the 2/6th battalions. From 1939-1944, all four Territorial battalions were assigned to the 59th (Staffordshire) Infantry Division, with the 1/6th having the distinction of being the regiment's first unit to go into action against German forces.

Of the regular battalions, men of the 1st saw action not only in North Africa, but also with the Chindits, and with the 77th Indian Infantry Brigade in Burma, where Lt. G. A. Cairns won the Victoria Cross. The 2nd South Staffs took part in the Sicilian Campaign, in which local names such as Dudley, Bilston and Walsall were used to indicate various objectives for airborne troops around Porto Grande, Syracuse. They also fought at Arnhem where Major R. H. Cain and Lance Sergeant J. D. Baskeyfield were both awarded the Victoria Cross.

As the war progressed further battalions were raised, of which the 12th and 13th became anti-aircraft units, the 14th an anti-tank battalion of the 6th Airborne. The 15th spent some time in the Faroes. There were a number of home defence battalions and a young soldiers battalion.

During the war the South Staffs earned 13 Battle Honours.

One of the prefabricated rail bars now
installed on the platforms of many British
railway stations, so that uniformed
passengers can quickly be served with tea
on their journeys.

"Jessie" carries the bags! 7th March 1944. Note the South Staffs crest on the cart.

The South Staffs on the march, January 1941.

Queen Wilhelmina of the Netherlands inspects Dutch Troops of the Princess Irene Brigade stationed at Wrottesley Hall & Park. Prince Bernhard is on the left of the picture carrying his baton horizontally. 29th August 1941.

Pioneers help clear the snow from Wolverhampton town centre, January, 1942.

Mechanics in RAOC divisional workshops repair cycles for immediate return to despatch riders, 5th December 1941.

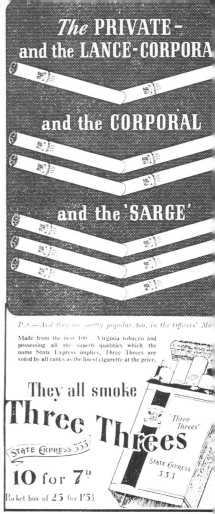
Open air catering!

AWKWARD MOMENTS

812 Coy Officers at the Officers Mess in Dorothy Round's house, Grange Rd., Dudley.

American forces are bearing down on Rommel's escape corridor.

Practice at loading an Anti-Aircraft gun, 16th December 1941. ⟶

For many weeks in succession the Mayoress (Mrs. B. T. Horwood, seen in centre) and a committee of

The King inspecting the 1/6th Bn, South Staffs Regt, composed of companies raised in the Black Country.

South Staffs. Regt. (MMG) participated in the liberation of Norway 1945.

WAAF recruits learn how to salute, on the march, by numbers! 22nd August 1941.

WAAF trainees at RAF Cosford

ATS drivers, January 1941

The Royal Air Force Comforts Committee

Voluntary Working Party Certificate

This is to Certify that the above-named Committee has been pleased to approve that

Mayor's Fund for Fighting Forces

be granted recognition as a Voluntary Working Party, Certificate Number *23 M.F.*, in recognition of their work for the Royal Air Force on active service.

Air Ministry

Date 3. 4. 42

Chairman,
Director of Personal Services

The WVS organise comforts for the Troops, Wolverhampton, 31st January 1940.

BLACK COUNTRY AIRFIELDS

RAF Cosford opened in August, 1938 as No. 2 School of Technical Training and during the war over 70,000 engine and airframe mechanics and armourers attended courses there. Cosford was also the home of the No. 9 Maintenance Unit whose main work was the preparation of Spitfires for front line use including a batch of 470 tropicalized for service in the Middle East. Two of their more unusual jobs were the preparation of 14 Blenheim bombers for the Rumanian Air Force and work on biplanes for the Finns. In July, 1941, No. 12 Ferry Pilots' Pool was formed to handle all Spitfire deliveries and 1943 it had the unique distinction of becoming the first all-woman ferry pool in the Air Transport Auxiliary. When the war ended Cosford was used to store surplus aircraft.

RAF Weston Park opened in October, 1940 as No. 33 Satellite Landing Ground and in June, 1941 Spitfires from Cosford were dispersed here. From early 1944 Weston Park was also used as a satellite by the Fleet Air Arm, who referred to it as HMS Godwit II.

RAF Perton was opened on 2nd August 1941 and was probably intended as a fighter station. However, the living quarters were handed over to the Princess Irene Brigade of the Royal Netherlands Army (who were also stationed in Wrottesley Park and Hall) and part of the base was used by Heliwells Ltd. for flight testing Boston and Havoc aircraft repaired by them at Walsall Airport. There was a plan to use Perton for parachute training but the closeness of a densely-populated area was seen as a security risk, and in any case the airfield suffered from too much industrial haze.

RAF Teddesley Park opened as No. 48 Satellite Landing Ground in July 1941. There were two 800-yard runways cut through the woods but pruning was kept to the absolute minimum in order to make the best possible use of the natural cover. Used as a storage site for aircraft from No. 29 Maintenance Unit at High Ercall, Teddesley Park, was closed early in 1946.

RAF Wolverhampton (Penderford) played host to the flight trials of the Boulton-Paul Defiant on 11th August 1937. The trials continued throughout 1938 but the second prototype did not fly until 18th May 1939. Boulton-Paul built 1060 Defiants and a further 105 Blackburn Rocs and 692 Barracudas under sub-contract. On 1st September 1941, No. 28 Elementary Flying Training School was established at Wolverhampton equipped with 30 Tiger Moths, though this was soon increased to 108 aircraft divided into six flights of 18 aircraft each.

Air space over Wolverhampton became so congested that Relief Landing Grounds were opened at Battlestead Hill and at Penkridge. During 1942 a group of officers from neutral Turkey arrived at Wolverhampton for training as part of a contract that had been won despite fierce competition from the Luftwaffe — all the more interesting when it is remembered that Turkey was on the verge of entering the war on the Axis side! By the end of the war Wolverhampton aerodrome had been reduced to giving refresher flying courses to RAF crews, though there was still a steady flow of foreign air force pilots being sent here for instruction.

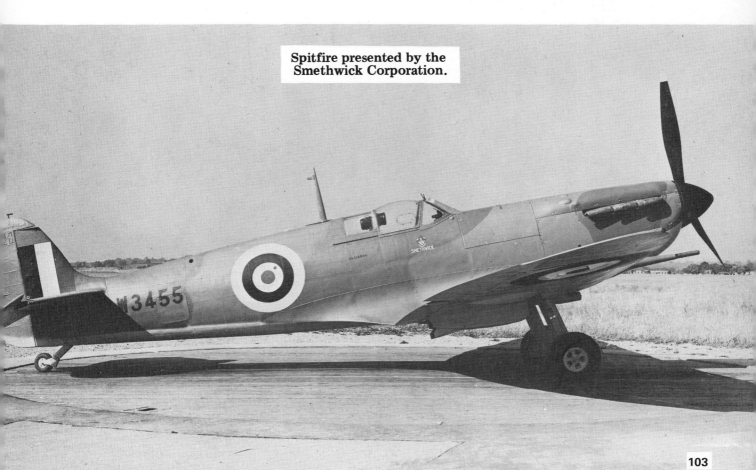

Spitfire presented by the Smethwick Corporation.

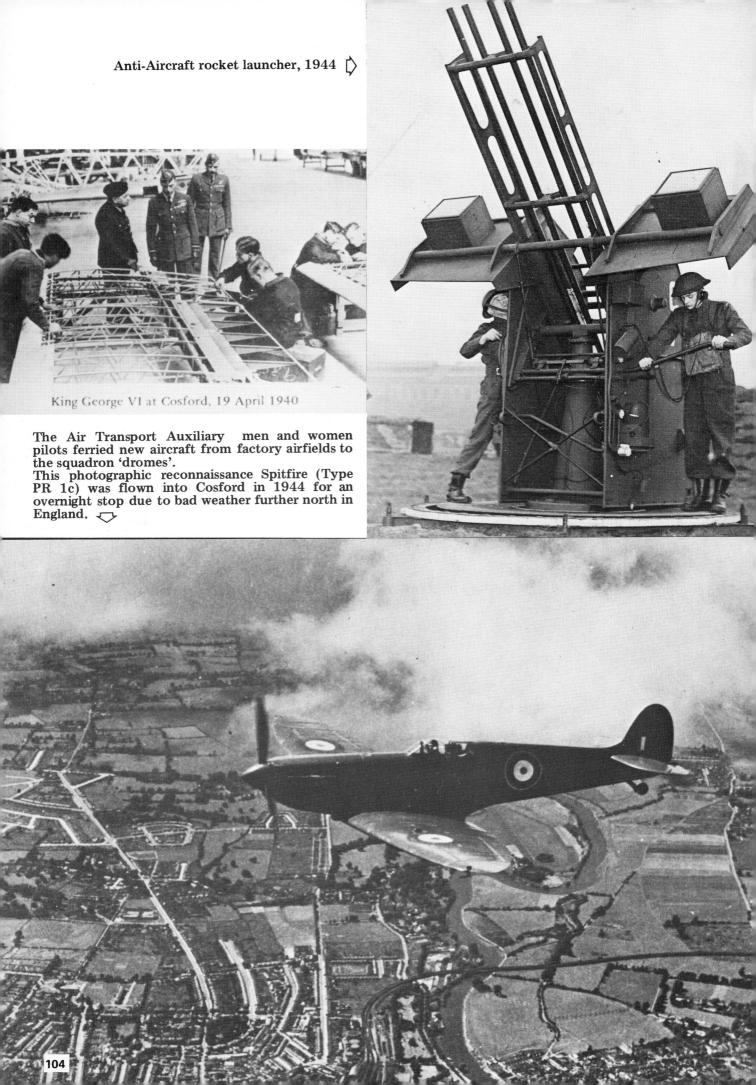

Anti-Aircraft rocket launcher, 1944 ▷

King George VI at Cosford, 19 April 1940

The Air Transport Auxiliary men and women pilots ferried new aircraft from factory airfields to the squadron 'dromes'.
This photographic reconnaissance Spitfire (Type PR 1c) was flown into Cosford in 1944 for an overnight stop due to bad weather further north in England. ▽

◁ RAF Cosford.
This splendid aerial photograph indicates just how well the art of camouflage can pay off. The 8 main hangars boast various mottled designs but the really clever dodge was the use of "creosote hedges", to disguise the actual airfield landing areas.
With a few exceptions, the aircraft dispersed around the environs of the airfield are Horsa Gliders of the type used at the Arnhem Drop and on D-Day.

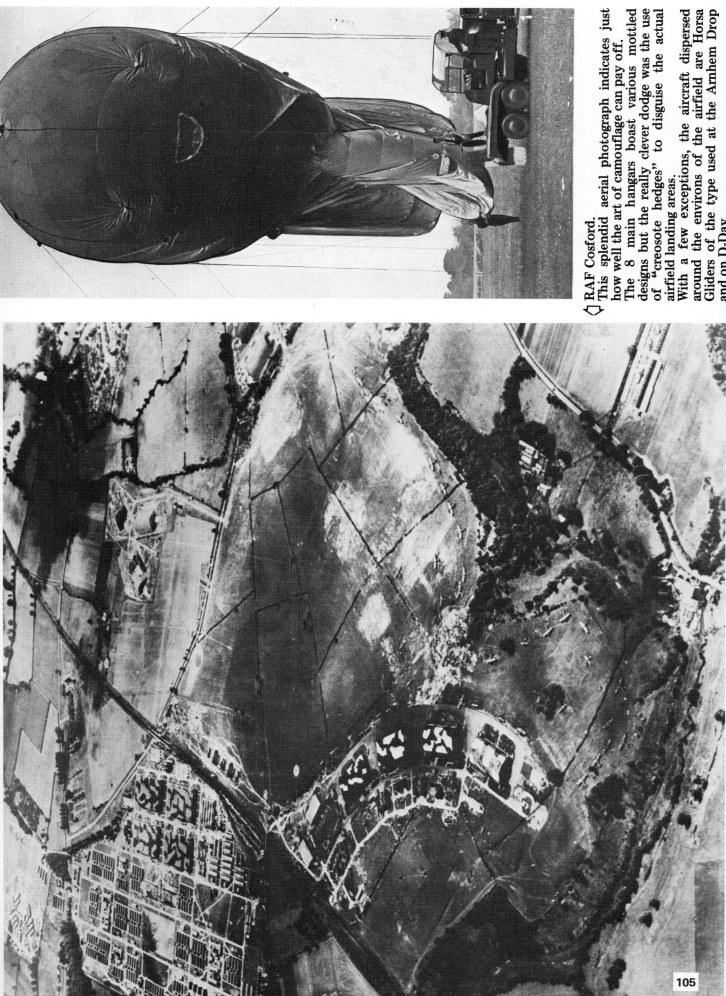

196 Air Defence Cadet Corps, now ATC, inspected by C.O., RAF Cosford, in late 1940 at Walsall Airport.

March past at the opening of Youth Week at Mary Stevens Park, Stourbridge, 2nd June 1945.

NAZIS SURRENDER TO MONTGOMERY

5-5-45.

ALL IN THE NORTH-WEST, HOLLAND AND DENMARK

1,000,000 INVOLVED

LAND, SEA AND AIR FORCES

All enemy forces in Holland, North-West Germany and Denmark, including Heligoland and the Friesian Islands, have unconditionally surrendered to Field-Marshal Montgomery's Twenty-first Army Group, it was officially announced last night. The surrender is effective from 8 a.m. to-day (British Double Summer Time).

More than a million Germans are involved in the surrender, according to correspondents. The plenipotentiaries included Admiral von Friedeberg (Commander-in-Chief of the German Navy in succession to Dönitz), General Dietel and Rear-Admiral Wagner (Chief of Staff to Friedeberg).

In the south, American Seventh Army troops have driven through the Brenner Pass into Italy and linked with the Fifth Army. Salzburg and Innsbruck, in Austria, have fallen.

Remnants of the German Ninth and Twelfth Armies surrendered to the United States Ninth Army yesterday.

HOW TERMS WERE SIGNED

The announcement of the surrender of the German forces on Field-Marshal Montgomery's front was made simultaneously at Supreme Headquarters and at 21st Army Group Headquarters (Reuter says). The text of the announcement, issued at 8.15 last night, was:—

Field-Marshal Montgomery reported to the Supreme Allied Commander that all enemy forces in Holland, North-West Germany and Denmark, including Heligoland and the Friesian Islands, have surrendered to 21st Army Group, to be effective at 8 a.m. (British Double Summer Time) to-morrow.

The troops in Denmark are estimated at 110,000, including 25,000 marines and other naval forces, and 17,000 airmen with ground staffs.

The German garrison in occupied Holland is estimated at about 80,000 strong.

The number of men involved in the surrender is well over 1,000,000, of whom 250,000 consist of naval personnel, it is learned authoritatively.

"Unconditional"

A B.U.P. correspondent at headquarters, describing the German surrender, said: "The time is ten minutes past six on Friday, the hour for which British fighting men and women, and British people throughout the world have been fighting and waiting and working for five years and six months. The commanders of the German forces opposing Field-Marshal Montgomery's 21st Army Group have come to his headquarters to-day to surrender.

"The plenipotentiaries are Admiral von Friedeberg, Commander-in-Chief of the German Navy, who succeeded Admiral Dönitz in that post when Dönitz became the new Führer. With him is General Dietel, Rear-Admiral Wagner (the Chief of Staff to von Friedeberg) and another staff officer. They came here yesterday to talk terms. They were told to go back and return to-day to make unconditional surrender. They have come back through the lines again to-day to make that surrender.

"No Arguments"

"Now they are walking up to the caravan the Field-Marshal uses for his headquarters in the field, and now von Friedeberg is entering the caravan. This was followed by Field-Marshal Montgomery's voice reading out terms of surrender. . . .

In North-West Germany, including the Friesian Islands and Heligoland and all other islands, in Schleswig-Holstein and in Denmark to the 21st Army Group. This will include all naval ships in those areas. These forces to lay down their arms and to surrender unconditionally.

All hostilities on land, on sea or in the air by German forces in the above areas to cease at 08.00 Double Summer Time on Saturday. The German Command to carry out at once and without argument or comments all further orders that will be issued by the Allied Powers on any subject. . . .

"Field-Marshal Montgomery continued:—

"'Disobedience of the orders or failure to comply with them will be regarded as a breach of the surrender terms and will be dealt with by the Allied Powers.

"'This instrument of surrender is independent of and without prejudice to and will be superseded by any general instrument of surrender imposed on behalf of the Allied Powers and applicable to Germany and the German armed forces as a whole.'"

The B.U.P. correspondent adds that the German representatives then signed in turn and Field-Marshal Montgomery signed on behalf of General Eisenhower.

Germans First Refused

A C.B.S. correspondent said that the surrender was signed at a headquarters set up by Field-Marshal Montgomery at the German Army training ground on the Luneberg Heath, south of Hamburg.

The German plenipotentiaries, when they arrived on Thursday, said they had come from Field-Marshal Busch " to ask you to accept the surrender of three German armies which are now withdrawing in front of the Russians in the Mecklenburg area."

Field-Marshal Montgomery replied: "Certainly not. Those German armies are fighting the Russians. Therefore, if they surrender to anyone, it must be to the forces of the Soviet Union."

The Germans at first refused to surrender the forces on Montgomery's northern and western flank and in Holland.

The Ultimatum

Later, Montgomery delivered his ultimatum. "You must understand three things," he said. "Firstly, you must surrender to me unconditionally all the German forces in Holland, Friedland and the Friesian Islands, and in Heligoland and all other islands and Schleswig-Holstein and in Denmark. Secondly, when you have done it, I am prepared to discuss with you the implications of your surrender. Thirdly, if you do not agree to surrender, then I will go on with the war and will be delighted to do so."

The Germans said they had no authority to agree to Montgomery's demands, but two of them went back to present the new terms of surrender to their superiors. They returned yesterday afternoon with the complete acceptance of the unconditional surrender terms.

Authoritative quarters at Field-Marshal Montgomery's headquarters last night emphasised the local nature of the surrender. Any further surrender on a wider scale is the province of the Supreme Commander himself.

Inability of the German Command on this front to control outlying units such as in Norway is believed to be the reason why the present surrender is not wider in scope.

It is officially stated that up to the last the German negotiators endeavoured to divide the Allies by offering surrender to the British but not to the Russians. This offer was resolutely refused by Montgomery, who insisted on total and unconditional surrender.

Field-Marshal Montgomery, it is disclosed, has never met Dönitz. The entire surrender negotiations have been conducted through Field-Marshal Busch and other German intermediaries.

◁ VE Party, Lewis Street, Bilston.

◁ VE Day view from Oldbury Town Hall. The Mayor, Councillor C. T. Barlow, has just laid a wreath on the War Memorial.

WESLEY PERRINS *(Wartime Councillor) "When the end of war was declared, one spontaneous gesture was that a great many of the local people flocked to Hodge Hill Methodist Church, Oakfield Road, Wollescote, Stourbridge, and held an impromptu service, led by a lay preacher, Noel Jeavons."*

VE Party, May 1945,
▷ Wheeler Street, Stourbridge.

COSELEY AND DISTRICT
PRISONERS OF WAR FAMILIES' CLUB
(Registered under the War Charities Act, 1940)

———

The Committee cordially invite you to the

Victory Dinner

to be served at the
BRITISH RESTAURANT
ON SATURDAY, THE 3RD NOVEMBER, 1945
AT 4.30 P.M. PROMPT.

———

The Chairman of the Council (Councillor G. W. H.
Turton, J.P.), will extend a Civic welcome, and will
be supported by Mr. Will Nally, M.P., Councillor
Edward Allen (Vice-Chairman of the Council) and
others.

———

The Dinner will be followed by a
GRAND VICTORY CONCERT
at Mount Pleasant Schools.

Queueing for oranges at Wolverhampton
wholesale market, December 1945.

Please God
OVER FOR EVER

Text of broadcast by the King on Germany's capitulation

TODAY we give thanks to God for a great deliverance.

Speaking from our Empire's oldest capital city, war-battered, but never for one moment daunted or dismayed—speaking from LONDON, I ask you to join with me in that act of thanksgiving.

GERMANY, who drove all Europe into war, has been finally overcome. In the Far East we have yet to deal with the Japanese, a determined and cruel foe. To this we shall turn with the utmost resolve and with all our resources.

But at this hour, when the dreadful shadow of war has passed far from our hearths and homes in these Islands, we may at last make one pause for thanksgiving, and then we must turn our thoughts to the tasks all over the world which peace in Europe brings with it.

FIRST let us remember those who will not come back; their constancy and courage in battle, their sacrifice and endurance in the face of a merciless enemy; let us remember the men in all the Services, the women in all the Services who have laid down their lives. We have come to the end of our tribulation, and they are not with us at the moment of our rejoicing.

Next let us salute in proud gratitude the great host of the living who have brought us to victory. I cannot praise them to the measure of each one's service, for in a total war the efforts of all rise to the same noble height, and all are devoted to the common purpose. Armed or unarmed, men and women, you have fought and striven and endured to your utmost.

None knows that better than I do, and as your King I thank with a full heart those who bore arms so valiantly on land and sea, or in the air, and all civilians who, shouldering their many burdens, have carried them unflinchingly and without complaint.

WITH those memories in our minds, let us think what it was that has upheld us through nearly six years of suffering and peril. The knowledge that everything was at stake; our freedom, our independence, our very existence as a people; but the knowledge also that in defending ourselves we were defending the liberties of the whole world; that our cause was the cause not of this nation only, not of this Empire and Commonwealth only, but of every land where freedom is cherished and law and liberty go hand in hand.

In the darkest hours we knew that the enslaved and isolated peoples of Europe looked to us; their hopes were our hopes; their confidence confirmed our faith. We knew that if we failed or faltered the last remaining barrier against a world-wide tyranny would have fallen in ruins.

But we did not falter, and we did not fail. We kept faith with ourselves and with one another; we kept faith and unity with our great Allies. That faith, that unity have carried us to victory through dangers which at times seemed overwhelming.

SO let us resolve to bring to the tasks which lie ahead the same high confidence in our mission. Much hard work awaits us both in the restoration of our own country after the ravages of war and in helping to restore peace and sanity to a shattered world.

This comes upon us at a time when we have all given of our best. For five long years and more, heart and brain, nerve and muscle have been directed upon the overthrow of Nazi tyranny. Now we turn, fortified by success, to deal with our last remaining foe.

The Queen and I know the ordeals which you have endured throughout the Commonwealth and Empire. We are proud to have shared some of them with you and we know also that we shall all face the future together with stern resolve and prove that our reserves of will-power and vitality are inexhaustible.

THERE is great comfort in the thought that the years of darkness and danger in which the children of our country have grown up are, please God, over for ever. We shall have failed, and the blood of our dearest will have flowed in vain, if the victory which they died to win does not lead to a lasting peace, founded on justice and established in good will.

To that, then, let us turn our thoughts on this day of just triumph and proud sorrow; and then take up our work again, resolved as a people to do nothing unworthy of those who died for us and to make the world such a world as they would have desired, for their children and for ours.

This is the task to which now honour binds us. In the hour of danger we humbly committed our cause into the Hand of God and He has been our Strength and Shield. Let us thank Him for His mercies and in this hour of Victory commit ourselves and our new task to the guidance of the same strong Hand.

ACKNOWLEDGEMENTS

(for providing anecdotes, memories, photographs,
encouragement and numerous other favours)

Dolly Allen; Geoff Allman; John Astley; Barry Balmayne; George Bartram; James Beattie; Joan Bennett; David Bills; Frank Bills; Bilston Library; Birmingham Post & Mail Ltd.; Black Country Museum; Black Country Society; Charlie Blackout; Blue Coat C. of E. School; Nan Bolland; E. L. Bouts; Pamela Bowden-Davies; Brierley Hill Library; John Brimble; Bertie Brown; Bundesarchiv, Koblenz; Anthea Burgess; Olive Caley; Dave Carpenter; Fred Carter; Ewart Cook; George Dennis; Dowty Group; Dudley Herald Ltd; Dudley Library; Ron Edwards; Everall Family; Express & Star Ltd.; L. Gordon Flint; Joe Gardiner; James Gibbons Ltd.; Goodyear Tyre & Rubber Co. (G.B. Ltd.); June & Dennis Granger; Edith Guest; John W. Harrison; Mitch Hickman; Betty Hodson; Joe Holmes; Robert Holmes; Margaret Horwill; John Huband; Imperial War Museum; Mike Inman; Mark Johnson; Christine & Richard Jones; James Kendall; Kinver Historical Society; Tony Matthews; Jim McKenzie; Metro Cammell Ltd.; Mitchells & Butlers Ltd.; Tommy Mundon; Philip Murphy; James Owen; Vera Parry; Sid & Gladys Pemberton; Wesley Perrins; John Phillips; RAF Cosford; Jenny & Bill Reeves; Harry Richards; Terry Roberts; Wynn Rumsey; Joe Russell; Sandwell Evening Mail Ltd.; Ida Shakespeare; Eddie Shepherd; Smethwick Library; Edgar Smith; George Smith; South Staffs Regt. Museum; Staffs County Record Office; Percy Stallard; Gordon Stretch; Thompson Tankers (NEI Thompson); Norman Taylor; Tipton Library; Irene Turley; Horace Vanes; Walsall Archives; Walsall F.C.; Walsall Observer; J. S. Webb; West Bromwich Albion F.C.; West Bromwich Library; Annie Westwood; David Whyley; Bert Williams; Harry Wilson; Ray Wilson; WMPTE; Fred Wollaston; Wolverhampton & Dudley Breweries Ltd.; WRVS; Joan Yusuf.

Please forgive any possible omissions. Every effort has been made to include all organisations and individuals involved in the book.